**Connect with English**

# Video Comprehension Book 2

Pamela McPartland-Fairman • Michael Berman • Linda Butler • Maggie Sokolik

McGraw-Hill

Boston, Massachusetts   Burr Ridge, Illinois   Dubuque, Iowa   Madison, Wisconsin
New York, New York   San Francisco, California   St. Louis, Missouri

# McGraw-Hill
*A Division of* The **McGraw·Hill** *Companies*

**CONNECT WITH ENGLISH: VIDEO COMPREHENSION BOOK 2**

Copyright © 1998 by the WGBH Educational Foundation and the Corporation for Public Broadcasting. All rights reserved. Printed in the United States of America. Except as permitted under the United States Copyright Act of 1976, no part of this publication may be reproduced or distributed in any form or by any means, or stored in a data base or retrieval system, without the prior written permission of the publisher.

This book is printed on acid-free paper.

domestic   1 2 3 4 5 6 7 8 9 0 QPD QPD 9 0 0 9 8 7
international   1 2 3 4 5 6 7 8 9 0 QPD QPD 9 0 0 9 8 7

ISBN 0-07-292758-5

*Editorial director:* Thalia Dorwick
*Publisher*: Tim Stookesberry
*Development editor:* Pam Tiberia
*Production supervisor:* Michelle Lyon
*Print materials consultant:* Marilyn Rosenthal
*Project manager:* Kate Gartner, Function Thru Form, Inc.
*Design and Electronic Production:* Function Thru Form, Inc.
*Typeface:* Frutiger
*Printer and Binder:* Quebecor Press Dubuque

Grateful acknowledgment is made for use of the following:

*Still photography:* Jeffrey Dunn, Ron Gordon, Judy Mason, Margaret Storm

*Additional photographs:* Episode 13 — Page 7 © A. Berliner / Gamma; Episode 24 — Page 7 left © Myrleen Ferguson / Photo Edit; 7 © Joseph Sohm / Photo Researchers

*Illustrations:* Episode 15 — p. 5, Janice Fried; Episode 18 — p. 7, 8, Andrew Shiff; Episode 19 — p. 7, Julie Durrell; Episode 20 — p. 3, Nick Jainschigg, p. 7, Lisa Goldrick; Episode 21 — p. 3, Nick Jainschigg, p. 7, Bill Colrus; Episode 22 — p. 5, Dave Sullivan, p. 7, Dave Sullivan; Episode 23 — p. 3, Nick Jainschigg

Library of Congress Catalog Card Number: 97-74213

**International Edition**
Copyright © 1998. Exclusive rights by The McGraw-Hill Companies, Inc., for manufacture and export.
This book cannot be re-exported from the country to which it is consigned by The McGraw-Hill Companies, Inc. The International Edition is not available in North America.

When ordering this title, use ISBN 0-07-115904-5.

http://www.mhhe.com

# TABLE OF CONTENTS

To the Teacher .................................................. v
A Visual Tour .................................................... vi
How to Use this Book ........................................ x
The Story So Far ............................................... xi

### EPISODE 13

#### Job Hunting
**Rebecca goes to the San Francisco College of Music. She gets some disappointing news.**

*Culture Focus: People of Different Cultures Living in the United States and Canada*

### EPISODE 14

#### A Bad Day
**Rebecca looks for a job in San Francisco. She receives a surprise phone call.**

*Culture Focus: Résumés*

### EPISODE 15

#### A Night Out
**Rebecca and Alberto go on a date. Alberto introduces Rebecca to his parents and his brother Ramón.**

*Culture Focus: Going on Dates*

### EPISODE 16

#### First Day of Class
**Rebecca starts classes at the San Francisco College of Music. She goes to another job interview.**

*Culture Focus: After-School Programs*

### EPISODE 17

#### Casey at the Bat
**Rebecca starts her new job at an after-school program. She speaks to her father on the phone.**

*Culture Focus: Using Titles*

### EPISODE 18

## The Art Gallery

**Rebecca goes to an art gallery with Alberto.
The Mendoza family talks about the future.**

*Culture Focus: Divorce*

### EPISODE 19

## The Picnic

**Ramón tells Rebecca about his problems.
There is some trouble at the after-school program picnic.**

*Culture Focus: Racism*

### EPISODE 20

## Prejudice

**A police officer talks to the children about the picnic.
Vincent tells his mother how he feels about the after-school program.**

*Culture Focus: The Police*

### EPISODE 21

## A Difficult Decision

**Mr. and Mrs. Wang make a decision about Vincent
and the after-school program.**

*Culture Focus: Computers*

### EPISODE 22

## Guitar Lessons

**Rebecca learns more about Ramón, his ex-wife, and Alex.
She also talks to the Wangs about guitar lessons.**

*Culture Focus: Watching Television*

### EPISODE 23

## The Retirement Party

**Ramón and Alex have a serious talk about Alex's mother. Friends and
family celebrate at the Mendozas' retirement party.**

*Culture Focus: Making Someone Comfortable*

### EPISODE 24

## The Phone Call

**While Rebecca is at the retirement party, she gets some bad news.
She leaves the party early.**

*Culture Focus: Retirement*

## Discussion Group Index
## Character Index

# TO THE TEACHER

The primary goal of each *Video Comprehension Book* is to help students build listening comprehension skills and gain a clear understanding of the characters and story line in the **Connect with English** video series.

This Introduction and the following Visual Tour provide important information on how each *Video Comprehension Book* and the corresponding video episodes can be successfully combined to teach English as a second or foreign language.

## PROFICIENCY LEVEL:

The comprehension exercises found in each *Video Comprehension Book* are accessible to high-beginning through intermediate students. While the majority of the activities are written at the high-beginning level, special *What About You?* features found throughout the books allow teachers to raise or lower the level of difficulty of the materials according to their students' abilities. These *What About You?* activities encourage students to share their personal opinions and ideas related to the characters and the story. Many times, students are asked to predict what they think will happen next. Because of the open-ended nature of these activities, there are numerous opportunities for classroom discussion and debates. The *What About You?* feature can also be used as the basis for writing and journal activities, creating further possibilities for exploration of themes related to the **Connect with English** story.

## LANGUAGE SKILLS:

The primary skill emphasized in each *Video Comprehension Book* is listening, along with recognition skills related to facial expressions, body language, and cultural nuances. Additional language skills/topics covered in each book include reading, oral communication, and vocabulary development.

## OPTIONS FOR USE:

Each *Video Comprehension Book* can be used in a variety of different learning environments, including classroom, distance learning, tutorial, and/or independent study situations. Instructors may choose to show the video during class time, while simultaneously using the *Video Comprehension Book*. If access to televisions or VCRs is not possible, teachers can assign students to watch the video episodes in a library, language lab, or at home. Class time can then be used for review of the activities found in the *Video Comprehension Book*.

The *Video Comprehension Books* can easily be combined with other corresponding texts in the **Connect with English** print program. For classes with an emphasis on oral communication skills, *Conversation Books 1-4* contain a variety of multi-level pair, group, team, and whole-class activities based on important themes and events from each episode. For classes with a focus on grammatical structures, *Grammar Guides 1-4* provide multi-level practice in grammar and vocabulary and also include various options for reading and writing activities. Finally, there are 16 *Connections Readers* which offer students graded reading practice based on the **Connect with English** story. For additional information about the **Connect with English** print program, please refer to the inside back cover of this book.

## A Visual Tour of this Text

This visual tour is designed to introduce the key features of *Video Comprehension Book 2*. The primary focus of each *Video Comprehension Book* is to help students develop listening and story comprehension. *Video Comprehension Book 2* corresponds to episodes 13–24 of *Connect with English*, and it presents an assortment of activities dealing with various aspects of comprehension, including understanding main points, comprehending details, ordering, decoding, inference, analysis, and more.

### The Opening Page
The first page of each chapter introduces key characters and themes from the corresponding video episode and builds on students' prior knowledge to help them predict upcoming events.

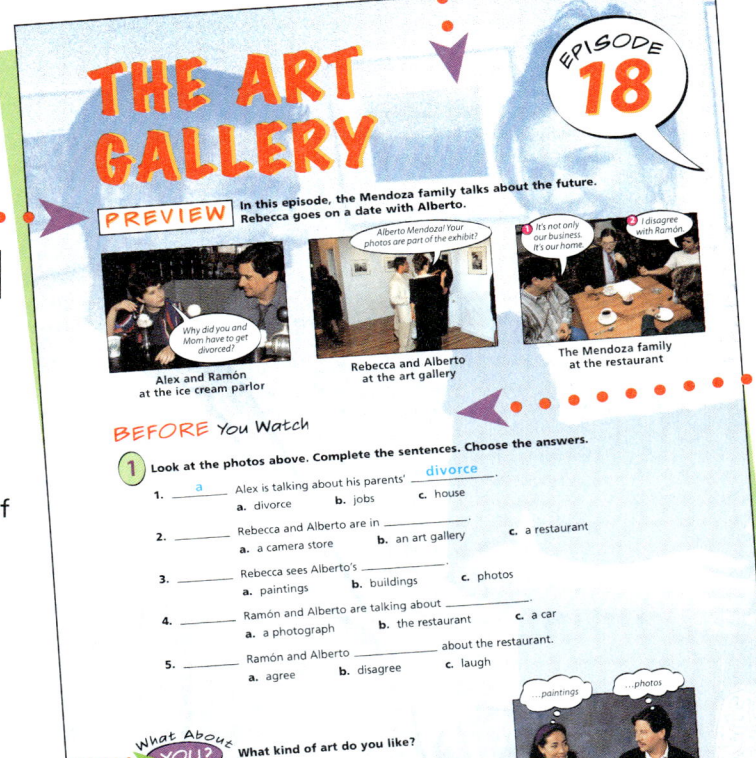

### PREVIEW
This section presents a brief summary of the video episode. The three photos highlight key events from each of the three parts of the episode. The **Preview** section builds students' confidence as it gives them a base of contextualized clues about the characters and story line before they watch the video.

### BEFORE You Watch
Activities in this section help students further identify the characters and story line. This particular example is a multiple choice activity which utilizes students' prior knowledge and calls upon their ability to make inferences about the information presented in the photos, captions, and speech bubbles on this page.

### What About YOU?
**What About You?** activities provide open-ended questions that encourage students to express their personal feelings, opinions, and reactions to the events and characters in the story. Whenever possible, language prompts or cues are used to provide linguistic support for lower-level students. At the same time, these activities create a springboard for more sophisticated discussions among students who are at higher levels of oral proficiency. The **What About You?** activities can also be used as optional writing assignments.

# WATCH FOR MAIN IDEAS

This first viewing activity asks students to watch the entire episode with the purpose of focusing on major story highlights.

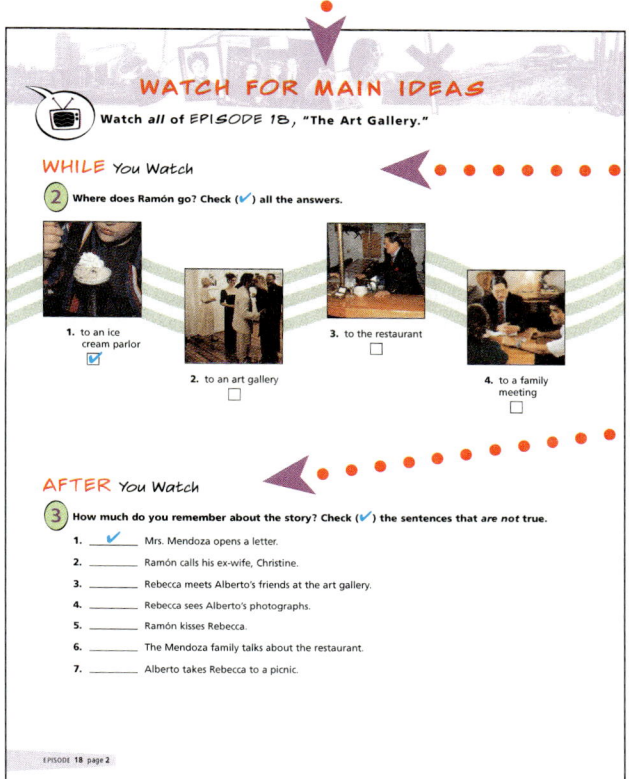

## WHILE You Watch

The **While You Watch** section provides a focused viewing activity dealing with specific people, places, things, and/or events central to the development of the story.

## AFTER You Watch

Activities in the **After You Watch** section ask students to recall specific information about the story. The first activity generally serves to check on students' comprehension of of the major events in the episode. Many of the activities in this section also include an emphasis on recognition skills for facial expressions, body language, and cultural nuances.

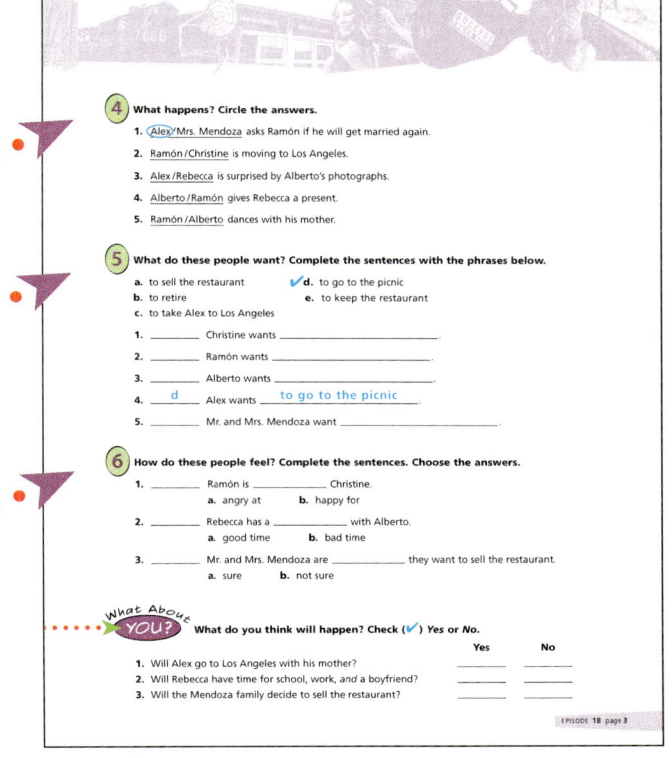

## Variety of Activity Types

A variety of different types of activities are included in each chapter, including multiple-choice, sentence completion, true/false, circling, and checking activities. The numbered activities are designed to be accessible to students engaged in independent study — at home, in a language lab, or any place where they have access to a TV and VCR. However, instructors can modify most of these activities into much more elaborate conversation and/or writing topics. For example, in the last sentence in Activity 6, we learn that the Mendozas are not sure that they want to sell the restaurant. In a classroom setting, instructors can start a discussion by simply asking the question, *"Why?"*

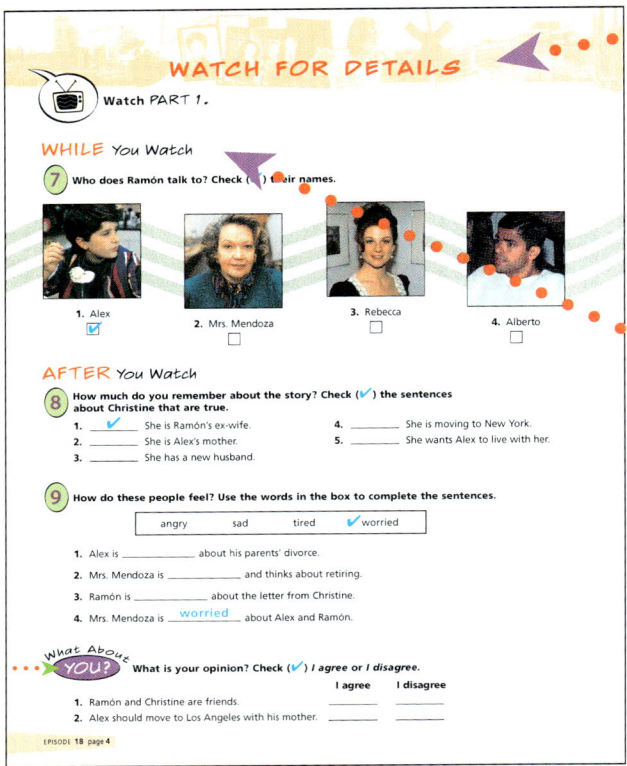

## WATCH FOR DETAILS

The **Watch for Details** section helps students develop a more specific understanding of the video story. Each video episode is divided into three viewing sections, labeled on-screen as Part 1, Part 2, and Part 3. In this section of the book, students are asked to view one part at a time, and comprehension is checked with more detailed activities regarding the characters and their experiences.

## WHILE You Watch

Many of the **While You Watch** activities in *Video Comprehension Book 2* require students to listen and watch carefully in order to identify speakers, key vocabulary, or completed actions or events. In this example, students listen for the titles of the photographs they see, giving them practice in listening for details.

## AFTER You Watch

The **After You Watch** activities continue to check students' comprehension of the story and help to solidify their understanding of the subtle nuances related to the characters' feelings and emotions.

## Discussion Topics Encourage Conversation

The **What About You?** activity shown here asks students to share their opinions on certain issues occurring in this episode. These questions can be used as a basis for in-class discussions related to the students' various cultures and how they compare with those shown in the video episode.

# HIGHLIGHTS

The **Highlights** page offers students an opportunity to explore various cultural and language points from the story.

# CULTURE

These boxes expand on subject matter found in the video by providing cultural information about life in the United States and Canada. In this example the topic of divorce is covered, as a few of the characters in this episode are experiencing divorce-related conflicts. An open-ended **What About You?** activity always follows the culture point and encourages students to compare and contrast their understanding of this new information with the corresponding cultural situation in their own countries.

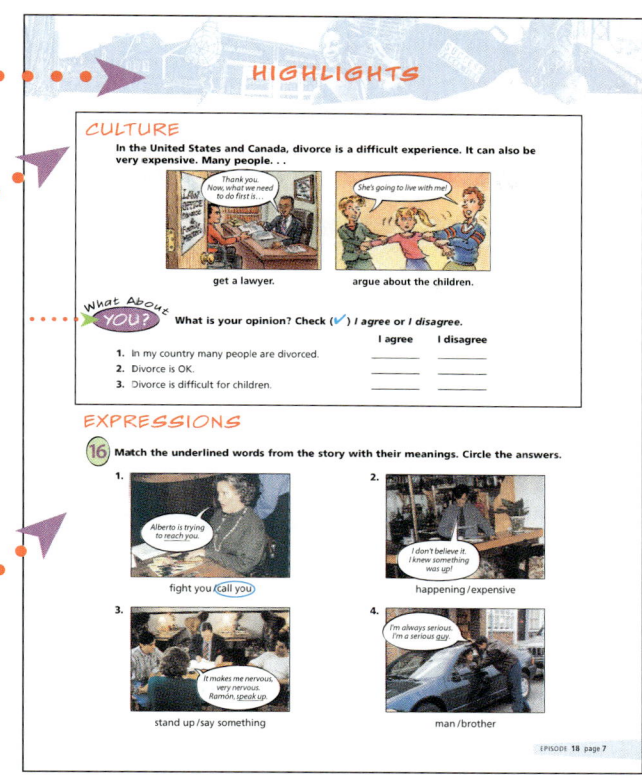

# EXPRESSIONS

In this section, students have an opportunity to work with some of the key idioms and expressions from the episode. Only those expressions which were presented in the context of the video story are included in this section. Care has been taken to ensure that the vocabulary features high-frequency items that students might encounter in conversational American English.

# REVIEW AND DISCUSS

This final page of each chapter gives students the opportunity to review the entire episode and offers a chapter-culminating discussion topic.

# STORY SUMMARY

In this section, students summarize the episode by selecting and inserting key vocabulary used in the video or earlier in the chapter. As in every exercise in the chapter, a sample answer is provided.

# VIEWPOINTS

Activities found in the **Viewpoints** section are based on the final review portion of the video episode. In this part of the video, various non-native English speakers from around the world talk about the episode and share their personal feelings about things that happened. Students using *Video Comprehension Book 2* are asked to interpret and react to these comments and ideas in a final **What About You?** activity.

# HOW TO USE THIS BOOK

**CONNECT WITH ENGLISH** is a story to help you learn English. Watch the program by yourself, in a classroom, or with family or friends. Record the program so you can watch it again. The episodes are closed-captioned. Turn on your caption system to see the words on the screen and get extra help in following the story.

This book will help you understand the story. Each episode has three parts. Before you watch the episode, look at the pictures in the *Preview* section. These pictures will show you some of the most important events from each part of the episode. The activities underneath the pictures will also help you get ready to watch.

Watch the episodes as many times as you need to. If you can, watch the whole episode one time through. Then you can go back and watch each part of the episode again. As you watch, you will see on-screen labels that say Part 1, Part 2, and Part 3. At the end of each episode, you will also see a group of students talk about the story.

The activities in the *Watch for the Main Ideas* and the *Watch for the Details* sections will help you learn the most important things that happen in each episode.

When you see a *What About You?* activity, you have a chance to talk about your own ideas and opinions about the **Connect with English** story. Discuss the questions and answers with your friends, family, or classmates. Your teacher might even ask you to write about your ideas.

In the *Highlights* section, a *Culture* box will tell you about life in the United States and Canada. In this section, you will also have a chance to talk about your country and how it is similar to or different from what you have learned about the United States and Canada. The *Expressions* section will help you understand some common American English phrases and expressions that the characters say in the episode.

On the last page of every chapter, a *Story Summary* reviews everything that happened in the episode. Look back through the activities you have already completed for help in doing the summary. The *Viewpoints* section gives you a chance to hear what some other English students think about **Connect with English**.

Remember, as you use this book, here's how you can *connect* with English: watch and record the episodes, read the book, and talk about the program with your family, friends, or classmates. Most of all, have fun and enjoy the story!

# THE STORY SO FAR

**1.** Rebecca Casey is a singer. Her dream is to go to music school.

**2.** Rebecca lives with her brother, Kevin, and her father, Patrick. Her mother is dead.

**3.** Rebecca's father doesn't want her to go to music school.

**4.** Rebecca's best friend is Sandy. Sandy's dream is to marry her boyfriend Jack and have a family.

**5.** Mr. Casey has some health problems. Rebecca is worried about her father.

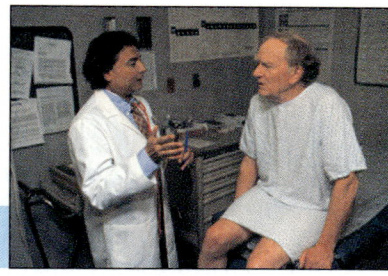
**6.** Rebecca is very happy when she is accepted to the San Francisco College of Music.

**7.** Rebecca and her boyfriend Matt end their relationship. They have different dreams.

**8.** Mr. Casey wants to help Rebecca. He buys her a car to drive across country.

**9.** Before Rebecca leaves for San Francisco, she tells Kevin that he has to help their father.

**10.** Rebecca's father says that he will miss her. He gives Rebecca her mother's necklace.

**11.** Rebecca's car breaks down in the desert. A man named Alberto helps her.

**12.** Rebecca's car costs too much to fix, so she sells it. Alberto wants to drive her to San Francisco. He lives there, too.

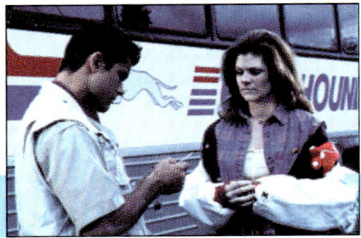
**13.** Rebecca takes the bus. Alberto wants to see her in San Francisco. She gives him her phone number.

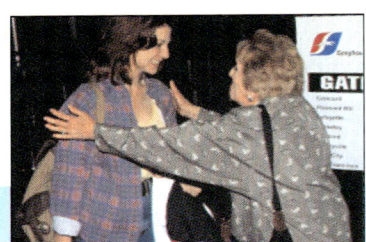
**14.** Rebecca meets her godmother, Nancy Shaw. Rebecca will stay with Nancy in San Francisco.

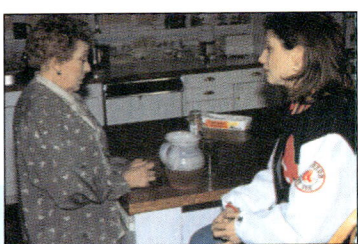
**15.** Rebecca is surprised when Nancy asks her to pay rent. Rebecca is worried about how she will pay her bills.

**LOOKING AHEAD** In this part of the story, Rebecca starts her new life in San Francisco. She goes to class at the San Francisco College of Music and gets a job at an after-school program. She sees Alberto again and meets two families that are very important to her.

**What About YOU?** What do you think will happen? Check (✔) *True* or *False*.

|  | True | False |
|---|---|---|
| **1.** Rebecca will fall in love with Alberto. | _____ | _____ |
| **2.** Rebecca won't like music school. | _____ | _____ |
| **3.** Kevin and Mr. Casey will miss Rebecca. | _____ | _____ |
| **4.** Sandy will move to San Francisco. | _____ | _____ |

# JOB HUNTING

**PREVIEW** In this episode, Rebecca is in her new home. She goes to the San Francisco College of Music to talk about a job.

Nancy and Rebecca at home

Angela and Melaku at home

María Gómez and Rebecca at the San Francisco College of Music

## BEFORE You Watch

**1** Look at the photos above. Circle the answers.

1. Nancy and Rebecca are at (Nancy's house) / a retirement home.
2. Nancy is happy / unhappy.
3. Melaku is going to pay the phone bill / rent.
4. Angela and Edward / Melaku pay rent on the first of the month.
5. María Gómez works at a restaurant / in an office.

**2** What happens to Rebecca at the college? Check (✓) the sentence that is true.

_____ a. She gets good news.
_____ b. She gets a good job.
_____ c. She gets bad news.

If you pay rent, how much do you pay?

I pay _____.

EPISODE 13   page 1

# WATCH FOR MAIN IDEAS

 Watch *all* of EPISODE 13, "Job Hunting."

## WHILE You Watch

 **Who does Rebecca talk to? Check (✔) their names.**

1. ___✔___ Melaku
2. _____ Kevin
3. _____ her father
4. _____ Nancy
5. _____ Angela
6. _____ María Gómez

## AFTER You Watch

 **How much do you remember about the story? Put the photos in order from 1 to 5.**

a. _____
b. _____
c. ___1___
d. _____
e. _____

a. *Anyway, how's Dad?*

b. *I'm here about my work-study arrangement.*

c. *I'd like to hear from the new arrival.*

d. ① *So what are your plans for today?* ② *I have a job interview at school.*

e. *Maybe he'll feel better next week.*

**What do you know about these people? Circle the answers.**

1. Angela / (Melaku) wants to start a business.
2. Angela / Melaku forgets that rent is due.
3. Angela / Rebecca doesn't find a job at her college.
4. Edward / Melaku lives in a retirement home.
5. Rebecca / Nancy says growing old is not easy.

 **What happens? Complete the sentences. Choose the answers.**

1. __a__ Rebecca drinks water because __the food is spicy__.
   a. the food is spicy
   b. there is no juice

2. _____ Nancy is sad because _____.
   a. Angela cannot pay rent
   b. Edward cannot come for dinner anymore

3. _____ Melaku has his _____.
   a. résumé
   b. rent money

4. _____ Rebecca is unhappy because _____.
   a. she doesn't have a job
   b. the bus stop is far from the house

 **What do you think will happen? Check (✔) Yes or No.**

|   | Yes | No |
|---|---|---|
| 1. Will Rebecca like her new home? | _____ | _____ |
| 2. Will Edward come back for dinner? | _____ | _____ |
| 3. Will Rebecca find a job? | _____ | _____ |

EPISODE 13  page 3

# WATCH FOR DETAILS

 Watch PART 1.

## WHILE You Watch

**7** Who is speaking? Write **R** for *Rebecca,* **N** for *Nancy,* or **M** for *Melaku.*

1. __M__ "Please watch out. This dish is very spicy."
2. _____ "You speak very well, Melaku."
3. _____ "I'll need it for my business someday."
4. _____ "Kevin, I have to go."
5. _____ "What's wrong, Nancy?"
6. _____ "I don't think Edward's going to come back for dinner."

## AFTER You Watch

**8** How much do you remember about the story? Circle the answers.

1. Who cooks the food? — Nancy / (Melaku)
2. Who is the "new arrival"? — Angela / Rebecca
3. Who does Rebecca talk to on the phone? — María / Kevin
4. Who can't come back to Nancy's house for dinner? — Edward / Angela
5. Who cries about Uncle Edward? — Nancy / Rebecca

**9** Check (✔) the sentences about Edward that are true.

1. __✔__ He corrects Angela's English.
2. _____ He likes to make jokes.
3. _____ He lives with Nancy.
4. _____ He asks Rebecca questions.
5. _____ He feels young and strong.

**What About YOU?** Check (✔) Yes or No.

|  | Yes | No |
|---|---|---|
| 1. Do you live with your family? | ____ | ____ |
| 2. Do you worry about people in your family? | ____ | ____ |

## Watch PART 2.

## WHILE You Watch

**10** Listen to Rebecca and Nancy's conversation. Circle the words they say.

1. Rebecca: "I have a class / job interview at school today."
2. Nancy: "Oh, that's why you look so nice /(business-like)."
3. Rebecca: "Do you think it's OK? I'm not quite sure what they expect / want."
4. Nancy: "It's fine. What kind of a job / scholarship are you applying for?"
5. Rebecca: "I don't know. I'm supposed to work at the factory / school to cover some of my tuition."
6. Nancy: "Oh. College is so expensive / cheap these days."

## AFTER You Watch

**11** How much do you remember about the story? Complete the sentences. Choose the answers.

1. __b__ Rebecca waits to use the __bathroom__.
   a. phone   b. bathroom   c. car

2. _____ Angela _____ new clothes.
   a. wears   b. needs   c. loses

3. _____ Nancy asks Angela to _____.
   a. cook dinner   b. clean the kitchen   c. pay rent

4. _____ Rebecca and Nancy talk about _____.
   a. Angela   b. Rebecca's father   c. college

5. _____ Rebecca has a _____ today.
   a. job interview   b. class   c. doctor's appointment

**12** What do you know about these people? Complete the sentences with the phrases below.

✓ a. goes to the library
  b. goes to school, then to a part-time job
  c. can pay the rent in a few days
  d. walks in the morning

1. _____ Angela _____.
2. __a__ Melaku __goes to the library_____.
3. _____ Nancy _____.
4. _____ Rebecca _____.

## Watch PART 3.

### WHILE You Watch

**13** Listen to Rebecca's job interview. Circle the answers.

1. María tells Rebecca that there is no class / job.
2. Rebecca is upset / happy.
3. María gives Rebecca a sample book / résumé to help her.
4. María tells Rebecca to look for another school / job.

### AFTER You Watch

**14** How much do you remember about the story? Check (✔) *True* or *False*.

|   | True | False |
|---|------|-------|
| 1. Rebecca received a letter from the college. |  | ✔ |
| 2. The college has a job for Rebecca. |  |  |
| 3. Rebecca still has some of her scholarship money. |  |  |
| 4. María is very sorry. |  |  |
| 5. Rebecca needs money for tuition, books, and rent. |  |  |
| 6. Rebecca can look for a job on the bulletin board. |  |  |
| 7. Rebecca has a résumé. |  |  |

**What About YOU?** What do you think will happen? Check (✔) *I agree* or *I disagree*.

|   | I agree | I disagree |
|---|---------|------------|
| 1. Rebecca will get a job. |  |  |
| 2. Rebecca will go back to Boston. |  |  |

# HIGHLIGHTS

## CULTURE

**People from many different cultures live in the United States and Canada. You can see these cultural differences in food, language, and music.**

food

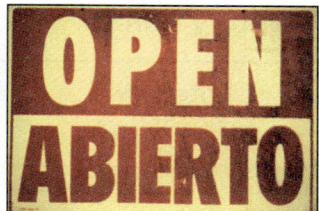
language

music

Check (✔) *Yes* or *No*.

|   | Yes | No |
|---|---|---|
| 1. Is it important to have many cultures in a country? | _____ | _____ |
| 2. Are there many cultures in your country? | _____ | _____ |

## EXPRESSIONS

 **Match the underlined words from the story with their meanings.**

a.

b.

c.

d.

1. ___c___ make him tired

2. _____ No.

3. _____ stopped working

4. _____ Be careful.

EPISODE **13** page 7

# REVIEW AND DISCUSS

## STORY SUMMARY

**16** Use the words in the box to complete the story summary for Episode 13.

| college | crying | ✔dinner | interview | job | needs |
|---------|--------|---------|-----------|-----|-------|
| phone | sad | strong | thanks | | worried |

Rebecca eats ___dinner___ (1) with Nancy, Edward, Melaku, and Angela. During dinner, Rebecca _____ (2) Nancy for her kindness. After dinner, Rebecca talks to Kevin on the _____ (3). Then she hears Nancy _____ (4). Nancy is _____ (5) because Uncle Edward is not _____ (6) enough to come for dinner anymore. Rebecca goes to the San Francisco College of Music for an _____ (7), but they do not have a _____ (8) for her. Rebecca is _____ (9). She _____ (10) a job to help pay for _____ (11), rent, and living expenses.

## VIEWPOINTS

**17** Watch the video discussion group. What does Rosalba mean? Complete the sentences. Choose the answers.

*I felt the same way.*

1. _____ Rosalba is talking about _____.
   
   a. Rebecca   b. Nancy   c. Edward   d. Melaku

2. _____ She is talking about _____.
   
   a. dinner   b. the hospital   c. culture shock   d. a date

Rosalba Solís, Mexico

### What About YOU?

What is your opinion? Check (✔) Yes or No.

|   | Yes | No |
|---|-----|----|
| 1. Do all people get culture shock when they move to a new country? | _____ | _____ |
| 2. Is it easy to live in a new city or country? | _____ | _____ |

# A BAD DAY

EPISODE 14

**PREVIEW** In this episode, Rebecca looks for a job. She talks with Angela and she sees Alberto again.

Rebecca
at a job interview

Rebecca and Angela
at home

Alberto and Rebecca
at Nancy's house

## BEFORE You Watch

**1** Look at the photos above. Check (✔) the sentences about Rebecca that are true.

1. __✔__ Rebecca goes to a job interview.
2. _____ She reads about the job in the newspaper.
3. _____ She tells Angela about her interviews.
4. _____ Angela tells Rebecca to go back to Boston.
5. _____ Alberto thinks Rebecca looks fat.

**2** Does Rebecca find a job? Check (✔) the answer.

_____ a. She doesn't get a job.

_____ b. She gets a job at a newspaper.

_____ c. She gets a job at an employment agency.

**What About YOU?** What is your opinion? Check (✔) Yes or No.

|  | Yes | No |
|---|---|---|
| 1. Are job interviews difficult? | _____ | _____ |
| 2. Are you nervous at job interviews? | _____ | _____ |

EPISODE 14 page 1

# WATCH FOR MAIN IDEAS

 Watch *all* of EPISODE 14, "A Bad Day."

## WHILE You Watch

 **3** Where does Rebecca go? Check (✔) all the answers.

**1.** an office building
✔

**2.** a factory
☐

**3.** Nancy's house
☐

**4.** Alberto's office
☐

## AFTER You Watch

 **4** How much do you remember about the story? Put the sentences in order from 1 to 5. Then write the sentences in the correct order below.

a. _____ Alberto calls Rebecca.
b. _____ Rebecca has a job interview at an office building.
c. _____ Angela and Rebecca talk at Nancy's house.
d. _____ Rebecca has a job interview at a factory.
e. __1__ Rebecca reads the want ads in the newspaper.

1. Rebecca reads the want ads in the newspaper.
2. _____
3. _____
4. _____
5. _____

**5** **What do these people do? Complete the sentences with the phrases below.**

a. interviews Rebecca for a job
b. shows Rebecca the city
✔ c. doesn't find a job
d. talks to Rebecca about her day

1. ___c___ Rebecca ___doesn't find a job___.
2. _____ Angela _____.
3. _____ Alberto _____.
4. _____ The boss at the factory _____.

**6** **What do you know about these people? Circle the answers.**

1. The man in the office building does /(doesn't) want to give Rebecca a job.
2. Rebecca is happy / tired after her interviews.
3. Angela thinks the job at the factory is good / bad.
4. Angela thinks Alberto is ugly / handsome.
5. Alberto thinks Rebecca is more beautiful / taller than before.

**What do you think will happen? Check (✔) Yes or No.**

|  | Yes | No |
|---|---|---|
| 1. Will Rebecca and Alberto fall in love? | _____ | _____ |
| 2. Will Rebecca have more job interviews? | _____ | _____ |
| 3. Will Rebecca find a job she likes? | _____ | _____ |

EPISODE 14 page 3

# WATCH FOR DETAILS

 Watch PART 1.

## WHILE You Watch

 Listen to Rebecca's interview at the factory. Check (✔) the sentences she says.

1. ✔ I'm organized.
2. ___ I'm a hard worker.
3. ___ What is the salary?
4. ___ I'll take the job.
5. ___ I say forget it.

## AFTER You Watch

**8** How much do you remember about the story? Check (✔) *True* or *False*.

|   | True | False |
|---|---|---|
| 1. Rebecca is looking for a part-time job. | ✔ | ___ |
| 2. Rebecca makes telephone calls because she wants a car. | ___ | ___ |
| 3. The man in the office wants someone who can use computers. | ___ | ___ |
| 4. Rebecca wants the job at the factory. | ___ | ___ |
| 5. Rebecca gets a job. | ___ | ___ |

**9** How does Rebecca feel? Complete the sentences. Choose the answer.

1. __c__  Rebecca feels __unhappy__ about her first two phone calls.

   a. happy     b. excited     c. unhappy

2. _____  Rebecca _____ the job in the office building.

   a. wants     b. doesn't want     c. gets

3. _____  Rebecca _____ the man at the factory.

   a. likes     b. doesn't like     c. hits

4. _____  Rebecca _____ her interviews.

   a. is happy with     b. is unhappy with     c. doesn't care about

# Watch PART 2.

## WHILE You Watch

**10** Listen to Angela talk to Rebecca. Circle the words Angela says.

1. "Hey, Rebecca. How was your  interview / (day)?"
2. "Was it that  good / bad ?"
3. "Oh, no. What are you going to  do / say ?"
4. "What about an employment agency? That's what  I / you  did."
5. "It's not  difficult / easy  to find a job."
6. "I was  lucky / sad  to find mine."

## AFTER You Watch

**11** How much do you remember about the story? Check (✔) the sentences that *are not* true.

1. __✔__ Rebecca has a lot of word processing skills.
2. _____ Angela says it's easy to find a job.
3. _____ Rebecca is happy about her interview at the factory.
4. _____ Alberto calls Rebecca.
5. _____ Rebecca and Alberto make a date.
6. _____ Alberto wants to show Rebecca the city.

**12** What do you know about Rebecca and Angela? Circle the answers.

1. (Rebecca) / Angela  has a bad day.
2. Rebecca / Angela  answers the want ads.
3. Rebecca / Angela  has a job.
4. Rebecca / Angela  hit someone.
5. Rebecca / Angela  lost her job.

 What is your opinion? Check (✔) *I agree* or *I disagree*.

|  | I agree | I disagree |
|---|---|---|
| 1. Sometimes I have a bad day. | _____ | _____ |
| 2. Looking for a job takes a long time. | _____ | _____ |

EPISODE **14** page 5

## Watch PART 3.

## WHILE You Watch

**13** Who is speaking? Write **A** for *Alberto*, or **R** for *Rebecca*.

1. __A__ "I'm here to see Rebecca Casey."
2. _____ "You look so different."
3. _____ "I could change back into my Red Sox jacket."
4. _____ "Are you going to tell me what it is?"
5. _____ "It's a surprise."

## AFTER You Watch

**14** How much do you remember about the story? Check (✔) the sentences about Alberto that are true.

1. _____ He meets Angela, Melaku, and Nancy.
2. _____ He thinks Rebecca looks the same as before.
3. _____ He wants Rebecca to put on her Red Sox jacket.
4. ___✔___ He is showing Rebecca San Francisco.
5. _____ He is taking Rebecca to breakfast.
6. _____ He has a surprise for Rebecca.

**15** How does Alberto feel? Check (✔) the answer that *is not* true.

*You look so...different!*

_____ a. He is surprised to see Rebecca in a dress.

_____ b. He is happy to see Rebecca.

_____ c. He is angry at Rebecca.

Where do you take visitors who come to your city?

I take them _____.

*...to a good restaurant*

*...to a great museum*

EPISODE **14** page 6

# HIGHLIGHTS

## CULTURE

In the United States and Canada, it can be very hard to find a job. To be successful, a person needs a good résumé.

A résumé tells about a person's education and work experience. Sometimes it describes a person's foreign language abilities, computer skills, and hobbies.

 What is your opinion? Check (✔) *I agree* or *I disagree*.

|  | I agree | I disagree |
|---|---|---|
| 1. A long résumé is better than a short résumé. | _____ | _____ |
| 2. Education is more important than work experience. | _____ | _____ |

## EXPRESSIONS

**16** Rewrite the sentences. Replace the underlined words from the story with their meanings.

    a. I understand
✔ b. Wait
    c. a little
    d. What happened?

1.
2.
3.
4.

1. __b__  Wait, I have to put in some more money.
2. _____  _____
3. _____  _____
4. _____  _____

EPISODE 14 page 7

# REVIEW AND DISCUSS

## STORY SUMMARY

**17** Use the words in the box to complete the story summary for Episode 14.

| calls | factory | feels | goes | hard | have |
|---|---|---|---|---|---|
| ✓ job | phone | see | skills | surprise | talks |

Rebecca reads the want ads for a __job__(1). She makes some _____(2) calls. She _____(3) to an interview, but she doesn't get the job. She needs more computer _____(4). Then Rebecca has an interview at a _____(5), but she leaves because she _____(6) uncomfortable. At home, Rebecca _____(7) to Angela. Angela tells Rebecca that it is _____(8) to find a job. Alberto _____(9) Rebecca. He invites her to _____(10) the city and to _____(11) dinner. He also has a _____(12) for Rebecca.

## VIEWPOINTS

**18** Watch the video discussion group. What does Boris mean? Check (✓) *True* or *False*.

*…I discovered that unless you have computer skills, you can't get anywhere.*

Boris Levitin, Russia

|  | True | False |
|---|---|---|
| 1. Boris understands Rebecca's problem. | _____ | _____ |
| 2. Boris thinks computer skills aren't important. | _____ | _____ |

 Check (✓) *Yes* or *No*.

|  | Yes | No |
|---|---|---|
| 1. Do you have computer skills? | _____ | _____ |
| 2. Are computer skills important in your country? | _____ | _____ |

# A NIGHT OUT

**EPISODE 15**

**PREVIEW** In this episode, Rebecca goes on a date with Alberto. She meets Alberto's mother, father, and brother.

*This place is magnificent.*

Alberto and Rebecca in San Francisco

*Papa, I'd like you to meet Rebecca Casey.*

Rebecca and the Mendozas at the restaurant

*Rebecca, this is my brother, Ramón.*

Ramón, Rebecca, and Alberto at the restaurant

## BEFORE You Watch

**1** Look at the photos above. Use the words in the box to complete the sentences.

| Alberto ✓dinner meets mother and father San Francisco |

1. Rebecca and _____ are on their first date.
2. First, Alberto shows Rebecca _____.
3. Then they have ____dinner____.
4. At the restaurant, Rebecca meets Alberto's _____.
5. Then Rebecca _____ Alberto's brother, Ramón.

How do you feel about first dates? Check (✓) *Yes* or *No*.

|  | Yes | No |
|---|---|---|
| 1. Were you ever nervous on a first date? | _____ | _____ |
| 2. Did you introduce your family on the first date? | _____ | _____ |

# WATCH FOR MAIN IDEAS

 Watch *all* of EPISODE 15, "A Night Out."

## WHILE You Watch

 **2** Who are these people? Circle their names.

1. (Alberto's mother) /
   Alberto's aunt

2. Alberto's boss /
   Alberto's father

3. Ramón / Alex

4. Ramón / Alex

## AFTER You Watch

 **3** How much do you remember about the story? Put the sentences in order from 1 to 7.

In the afternoon...

a. _____ Rebecca sings a song.

b. ___1___ Alberto shows Rebecca a special building.

c. _____ Alberto and Rebecca go to the Golden Gate Bridge.

In the evening...

d. _____ Rebecca talks with Ramón.

e. _____ Rebecca and Alberto order their food.

f. _____ Alberto takes Rebecca home.

g. _____ Alberto introduces his parents to Rebecca.

**4** What do you know about these people? Complete the sentences with the phrases below.

a. sings for Alberto
b. tells Rebecca about a job
c. is an architect
d. own the Casa Mendoza restaurant
e. needs a job

1. __a__ Rebecca __sings for Alberto__.
2. _____ Rebecca _____.
3. _____ Alberto _____.
4. _____ Ramón _____.
5. _____ Mr. and Mrs. Mendoza _____.

**5** What do you know about the Mendoza family? Check (✔) *True* or *False*.

|  | True | False |
|---|---|---|
| 1. The Casa Mendoza restaurant is an Italian restaurant. | _____ | ✔ |
| 2. Ramón works at the restaurant. | _____ | _____ |
| 3. Rebecca talks to Alex. | _____ | _____ |
| 4. Ramón wants Rebecca to work in the restaurant. | _____ | _____ |
| 5. The Mendoza family speaks Spanish. | _____ | _____ |

**What About YOU?** What do you think will happen? Check (✔) *I agree* or *I disagree*.

|  | I agree | I disagree |
|---|---|---|
| 1. Alberto will see Rebecca again. | _____ | _____ |
| 2. Rebecca will want to go on another date with Alberto. | _____ | _____ |
| 3. Rebecca will find a job. | _____ | _____ |

EPISODE **15** page 3

# WATCH FOR DETAILS

 Watch PART 1.

## WHILE You Watch

 **6** Listen to Rebecca's song. Circle the words she sings.

1. "Go to sleep / bed.
2. The stars / lights are brightly shining.
3. Go to sleep / bed.
4. The night / moon is on the rise.
5. Our life's a job / dream.
6. We barely know / see we're dreaming.
7. Till I see the star / light that's shining in your eyes.
8. Till I see the light that's shining in your heart / eyes."

## AFTER You Watch

 **7** How much do you remember about the story? Complete the sentences. Choose the answers.

1. __a__ Alberto _designed this building_.
   a. designed this building
   b. lives in this building
   c. works in this building

2. _____ This building is _____.
   a. old
   b. new
   c. in Boston

3. _____ This is _____.
   a. Alberto's house
   b. the Palace of Fine Arts
   c. the Mendozas' restaurant

4. _____ Alberto and Rebecca _____.
   a. read about it
   b. go there
   c. don't go there

5. _____ Rebecca tells Alberto _____.
   a. about her family
   b. about her interviews
   c. about Uncle Edward

6. _____ Rebecca's song is from her _____.
   a. music teacher
   b. father
   c. mother

 **Watch PART 2.**

## WHILE You Watch

**8** Listen to Rebecca and Alberto in the restaurant. Circle what they order for dinner.

Casa Mendoza's Dinner Menu
cheese enchiladas ... $12.95
chicken enchiladas ... $13.50
chili poblano relleno ... $13.50
grilled shrimp ... $14.95
tacos ... $9.95
nachos ... $9.50
salad ... $6.75
soup ... $5.25

## AFTER You Watch

 **9** How much do you remember about the story? Circle the answers.

1. Who knows a good restaurant? — Rebecca / **Alberto**
2. Who are retiring soon? — Alberto's parents / Alberto and Ramón
3. Who wants Alberto to work in the restaurant? — Mr. Mendoza / Rebecca
4. Who recommends the chicken enchiladas? — Alberto / Mr. Mendoza
5. Who says Rebecca is pretty? — Mr. Mendoza / Mrs. Mendoza

 **10** Read what Rebecca says. How does she feel? Circle the answers.

1. She says, "It's beautiful, the way the light hits the buildings."
   She is <u>happy</u> / worried.

2. She says, "Good, I love Mexican food."
   She is bored / <u>excited</u>.

3. She says, "I didn't expect to meet your parents!"
   She is happy / <u>nervous</u>.

 **What is your opinion?**

Does Alberto like Rebecca?
How do you know?

I know because _____

...he smiles at her
...he looks at her
...he holds her hand

EPISODE 15  page 5

 **Watch PART 3.**

## WHILE You Watch

**11** **What does Ramón tell Rebecca? Circle the words he says.**
1. "Maybe you can give (guitar)/ piano lessons to my son."
2. "He's twelve / ten."
3. "They're looking for someone at Alex's after-school / in-school program."
4. "I'll give you the teacher's / director's phone number."

## AFTER You Watch

**12** **How much do you remember about the story? Complete the sentences. Choose the answers.**

1. __b__ Rebecca meets __Ramón__.
   a. Alex    b. Ramón    c. Alberto

2. _____ Ramón has a picture of his _____.
   a. son    b. nephew    c. wife

3. _____ Rebecca says she is trying to pay for _____.
   a. dinner    b. guitar lessons    c. music school

4. _____ Ramón tells Rebecca about _____.
   a. Mexico    b. San Francisco    c. a job

5. _____ _____ takes Rebecca home.
   a. Ramón    b. Alberto    c. Mr. Mendoza

**13** **Check (✔) the sentences about Ramón that are true.**
1. __✔__ He wants his son to take music lessons.
2. _____ His son, Alex, is sixteen years old.
3. _____ He manages the Casa Mendoza restaurant.
4. _____ He has a son and a daughter.
5. _____ He gives Rebecca a phone number.

 **What is your opinion? Check (✔) True or False.**

|  | True | False |
|---|---|---|
| 1. Ramón is older than Alberto. | _____ | _____ |
| 2. Ramón works hard. | _____ | _____ |
| 3. Ramón and Alberto have a good relationship. | _____ | _____ |

# HIGHLIGHTS

## CULTURE

In the United States and Canada, people do many different things on dates.

**What About YOU?** What do you like to do on a date? Check (✔) your answers.

I like to _____.

_____ go to a movie          _____ hold hands
_____ go to a restaurant     _____ dance
_____ walk                    _____ go to a rock concert
_____ talk                    _____ play sports

Some dates are formal. Other dates are informal.

## EXPRESSIONS

 **Match the underlined words from the story with their meanings. Circle the answers.**

1. ① Would you like to go see the Golden Gate Bridge?
   ② I'd love to.

   a. I love bridges.
   b. **I really want to.** (circled)

2. ① Are you ready for dinner?
   ② I'm starving.

   a. I'm very hungry.
   b. I'm not hungry.

3. ① Hello, it's a pleasure to meet you.
   ② How do you do?

   a. What do you do?
   b. It's nice to meet you.

4. I found out I have an early meeting tomorrow.

   a. I learned
   b. I told them

# REVIEW AND DISCUSS

## STORY SUMMARY

**15** Use the words in the box to complete the story summary for Episode 15.

| brother | call | ✔ city | dinner | go | her | home | job |
|---------|------|--------|--------|-----|-----|------|-----|
| meets | program | restaurant | shows | sings | son | takes | |

Alberto gives Rebecca a tour of the ___city___ (1). First he _____ (2) her a building that he helped design. Then he takes _____ (3) to the Palace of Fine Arts. Rebecca _____ (4) a song. Next they _____ (5) to the Golden Gate Bridge. Alberto _____ (6) Rebecca to the Casa Mendoza _____ (7) for dinner. Rebecca _____ (8) Alberto's mother and father and his _____ (9), Ramón. Ramón shows Rebecca a picture of his _____ (10), Alex. Ramón tells Rebecca to _____ (11) Alex's after-school _____ (12) for a _____ (13). After dinner, Alberto takes Rebecca _____ (14). She thanks him for _____ (15) and the tour.

## VIEWPOINTS

**16** Watch the video discussion group. Who are the students describing? Check (✔) the answers.

Hai B. Pho

1. Hai: "He's a sensible family man, a very stable person."
   **Alberto**   **Ramón**
   _____   _____

Nela Hosic

2. Nela: "I think he's more responsible."
   **Alberto**   **Ramón**
   _____   _____

3. Nela: "He's more carefree."
   **Alberto**   **Ramón**
   _____   _____

 **What About YOU?** What is your opinion? Check (✔) *Yes* or *No*.

|  | Yes | No |
|---|---|---|
| 1. Is Ramón more responsible than Alberto? | _____ | _____ |
| 2. Is Ramón a better son than Alberto? | _____ | _____ |

# FIRST DAY OF CLASS

EPISODE 16

**PREVIEW** In this episode, Rebecca meets Bill Ellis and Emma Washington. Ramón Mendoza and his mother have a serious conversation.

Rebecca and Bill Ellis at school

Rebecca and Emma Washington at the after-school program

Ramón and his mother at the restaurant

## BEFORE You Watch

**1** Look at the photos above. Complete the sentences. Choose the answers.

1. __c__ Rebecca and Bill are at __the music school__.
   a. Nancy's house   b. a restaurant   c. the music school
2. _____ Music school is _____.
   a. easy   b. hard   c. cheap
3. _____ Rebecca goes to _____.
   a. an interview   b. a bank   c. a movie
4. _____ Rebecca wants a _____ from Emma Washington.
   a. good grade   b. résumé   c. job
5. _____ Mrs. Mendoza is _____ about Ramón.
   a. happy   b. worried   c. laughing

What is your opinion?

School can be hard because _____.

EPISODE 16 page 1

# WATCH FOR MAIN IDEAS

 Watch *all* of EPISODE 16, "First Day of Class."

## WHILE You Watch

**2** Who are these people? Circle their names.

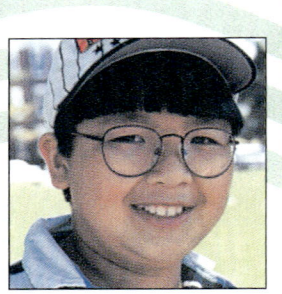

1. (Bill) / Vincent
2. Emma / Tanya
3. Alex / Vincent
4. Alex / Vincent
5. Mr. Mendoza / Mr. Wang

## AFTER You Watch

**3** How much do you remember about the story? Put the photos in order from 1 to 5.

a. _____
b. _____
c. _____
d. _____
e. ___1___

a. *Miss Casey, this is Alex Mendoza. This is Vincent Wang.*

b. *They want to buy the restaurant.*

c. *Both will suffer — your son and the restaurant.*

d. *I need a job.*

e. *By the way, I'm Bill Ellis.*

**4** What do you know about these people? Circle the answers.

1. Bill and Rebecca  (think) / don't think  their class is hard.
2. Bill wants to  have dinner / study  with Rebecca.
3. María Gómez asks Rebecca for  money / help  for music school.
4. Emma Washington  talks / doesn't talk  to Rebecca.
5. Alex and Vincent are  brothers / friends.
6. Alberto talks to Ramón about  Rebecca / the restaurant.
7. The restaurant is  important / not important  to Ramón.

**5** What do you know about these people? Complete the sentences. Choose the answers.

1. _____ Ramón, Alberto, and their mother _____.
   a. always agree    b. sometimes disagree    c. never talk.
2. ___a___ Rebecca is _____happy_____ that she meets Bill.
   a. happy    b. sad    c. angry
3. _____ Ramón loves _____.
   a. only the restaurant    b. only his son    c. his son and the restaurant
4. _____ Emma Washington tells Rebecca about _____.
   a. the job    b. the restaurant    c. music school
5. _____ Rebecca _____ the job.
   a. wants    b. doesn't want    c. doesn't need

**What About YOU?** What do you think will happen? Check (✔) Yes or No.

|  | Yes | No |
|---|---|---|
| 1. Will Rebecca study with Bill? | ____ | ____ |
| 2. Will Rebecca get a job at the after-school program? | ____ | ____ |
| 3. Will Ramón quit the restaurant? | ____ | ____ |

# WATCH FOR DETAILS

 **Watch PART 1.**

## WHILE You Watch

**6** Who is speaking? Write **R** for *Rebecca,* **B** for *Bill,* or **M** for *María Gómez.*

1. _____ "Do you want to meet in the student lounge . . . ?"
2. _____ "Oh, I can't today."
3. _____ "Here's my phone number . . ."
4. __M__ "We'll need a check for the rest by Friday."
5. _____ "It's going to be tough."
6. _____ "Maybe we should start you on a payment plan."

## AFTER You Watch

**7** How much do you remember about the story? Check (✔) *True* or *False*.

|  | True | False |
|---|---|---|
| 1. Professor Thomas's class is easy. | _____ | ✔ |
| 2. Bill asks Rebecca to study. | _____ | _____ |
| 3. Rebecca doesn't want to study with Bill. | _____ | _____ |
| 4. Rebecca has a job interview. | _____ | _____ |
| 5. María starts a payment plan for Rebecca. | _____ | _____ |

**8** What do you know about these people? Complete the sentences with the phrases below.

a. wants a job
b. gives Rebecca some forms
c. gives Rebecca his phone number
d. is a music teacher

1. __d__ Professor Thomas __is a music teacher__.
2. _____ Bill _____.
3. _____ Rebecca _____.
4. _____ María Gómez _____.

**Watch PART 2.**

## WHILE You Watch

**9** Listen to Rebecca talk with Emma. Circle the words Rebecca says.

1. "I love working with (children) / money."
2. "I have a lot of time / experience."
3. "I can sing / dance."
4. "I can play the violin / guitar."
5. "I need some money / a job."

## AFTER You Watch

**10** How much do you remember about the story? Put the sentences in order from 1 to 5. Then write the sentences in the correct order below.

a. _____ Rebecca and Emma talk about Alex Mendoza.
b. _____ Rebecca asks about money.
c. _____ Emma reads Rebecca's résumé.
d. ___1___ Rebecca finds Emma Washington's office.
e. _____ Rebecca meets Emma.

1. __Rebecca finds Emma Washington's office.__
2. _____
3. _____
4. _____
5. _____

**What About YOU?** What is your opinion? Check (✔) *True* or *False*.

|  | True | False |
|---|---|---|
| 1. I like children. | _____ | _____ |
| 2. I like to work with children. | _____ | _____ |
| 3. Working with children is easy. | _____ | _____ |

## Watch PART 3.

### WHILE You Watch

**11** Where are these people? Complete the sentences. Choose the answers.

1. _____ Ramón and his mother are at the _____.
   a. restaurant     b. after-school program

2. _____ Alex and Rebecca are at the _____.
   a. restaurant     b. after-school program

3. _____ Alberto and Ramón are _____.
   a. at Alberto's office     b. in front of the restaurant

### AFTER You Watch

**12** How much do you remember about the story? Circle the answers.

1. Who talks to Ramón about his son?          Alberto / (Mrs. Mendoza)
2. Who is the guitar teacher?                 Rebecca / Emma
3. Who wants to be a rock star?               Alex / Emma
4. Who doesn't want to sell the restaurant?   Alberto / Ramón
5. Who does Rebecca meet?                     Mr. Wang / María Gómez

**13** Who do these sentences describe? Write **A** for *Alberto,* or **R** for *Ramón.*

1. __R__ He runs the restaurant.
2. ____ He is going to pick up Alex.
3. ____ He wants to sell the restaurant.
4. ____ He thinks money is very important.
5. ____ He thinks the restaurant is very important.
6. ____ He wants to have a family meeting.

### What About YOU?

What is your opinion? Check (✓) *I agree* or *I disagree.*

|   | I agree | I disagree |
|---|---------|------------|
| 1. Ramón is a good father. | _____ | _____ |
| 2. Ramón should sell the restaurant. | _____ | _____ |

# HIGHLIGHTS

## CULTURE

In the United States and Canada, after-school programs and day-care centers are very popular. These programs help parents. Then parents can work while their children play.

 Check (✔) *Yes* or *No*.

|  | Yes | No |
|---|---|---|
| 1. Are after-school programs/day-care centers popular in your country? | _____ | _____ |
| 2. Is an after-school program a good place for children? | _____ | _____ |

## EXPRESSIONS

 **Match the underlined words from the story with their meanings.**

1. ___d___ Not good, not bad.
2. _____ review
3. _____ complete these
4. _____ come in a moment

a.

b.

c.

d.

# REVIEW AND DISCUSS

## STORY SUMMARY

**15** Use the words in the box to complete the story summary for Episode 16.

| buy | check | class | director | hard | interview |
|---|---|---|---|---|---|
| ✔ meets | plan | sell | study | talks | tells |

At school, Rebecca ___meets___ (1) Bill Ellis. They are in the same _____ (2). Bill wants to _____ (3) with Rebecca because their class is _____ (4). Rebecca also talks to María Gómez. María asks Rebecca for a _____ (5) to pay for school. It's a lot of money, so Rebecca decides to start a payment _____ (6). Later, Rebecca has an _____ (7) at Alex's after-school program. Rebecca talks to the _____ (8), Emma Washington. Emma _____ (9) Rebecca about the job. After the interview, Rebecca meets Vincent and Alex. At the restaurant, Alberto _____ (10) to Ramón. Some people want to _____ (11) the restaurant. Ramón doesn't want to _____ (12) it.

## VIEWPOINTS

**16** Watch the video discussion group. Complete the sentences. Choose the answers.

1. _____ Ventha is talking about _____.
   a. Mr. Wang    b. Ramón    c. Alex

2. _____ Ventha thinks it's a good idea to _____.
   a. sell the restaurant    b. retire    c. keep the restaurant

*I'd rather keep the business if it were me.*

Ventha Danapalan, India

### What About YOU?

What is your opinion? Check (✔) *I agree* or *I disagree*.

|   | I agree | I disagree |
|---|---|---|
| 1. The Mendoza family should sell the restaurant. | _____ | _____ |
| 2. Alberto should work with Ramón at the restaurant. | _____ | _____ |

# CASEY AT THE BAT

**EPISODE 17**

**PREVIEW** In this episode, Rebecca starts her new job. She talks with her father and with Ramón and Alex Mendoza.

Ramón, Alex, and Rebecca at the after-school program

1. I got the job! Thanks for telling me about it.
2. You're welcome.

Rebecca and her father on the phone

1. Are you all right?
2. Like I said, I'm fine.

Ramón and Alex at the after-school program

1. Miss Casey knows Uncle Alberto?
2. Yes, they're friends.

## BEFORE You Watch

**1** Look at the photos above. Circle the answers.

1. Rebecca gets the job at the <u>after-school program</u>/restaurant.
2. <u>Alberto</u>/Ramón helps Rebecca get the job.
3. Rebecca is sad/<u>happy</u> about getting a job.
4. Rebecca is happy/<u>worried</u> about her father's health.
5. Ramón tells Alex that Rebecca and <u>Alberto</u>/Bill are friends.

**2** What do you know about Mr. Casey? Check (✔) the answer.

_____ a. He visits Rebecca in San Francisco.
_____ b. He tells Rebecca how he is feeling.
_____ c. He tells Rebecca he is happy about her new job.

 What is your opinion? Check (✔) Yes or No.

|  | Yes | No |
|---|---|---|
| 1. Will Rebecca like her new job? | _____ | _____ |
| 2. Is Rebecca's father really OK? | _____ | _____ |

# WATCH FOR MAIN IDEAS

 Watch *all* of EPISODE 17, "Casey at the Bat."

## WHILE You Watch

**3** Who talks to Rebecca? Check (✔) all the answers.

1. ✔ Emma
2. _____ Alex
3. _____ Ramón
4. _____ Nancy
5. _____ Mr. Casey
6. _____ Kevin
7. _____ Melaku
8. _____ Alberto

## AFTER You Watch

**4** How much do you remember about the story? Put the sentences in order from 1 to 8.

a. _____ Alex practices his spelling with Rebecca.
b. _____ Ramón arrives at the after-school program.
c. __1__ Rebecca gets the job.

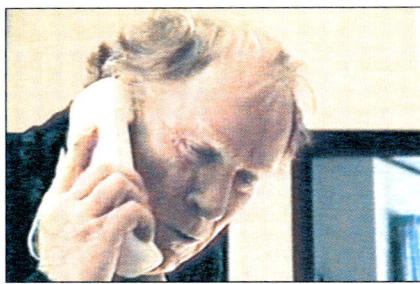

d. _____ Rebecca gets flowers.
e. _____ Rebecca asks her father if he is OK.

f. _____ Ramón and Alex talk about guitar lessons.
g. _____ Rebecca plays softball with the children.
h. _____ Alberto talks to Rebecca.

## 5. What do you know about Rebecca? Check (✔) *True* or *False*.

|   | True | False |
|---|---|---|
| 1. Her father is sick. | ✔ | |
| 2. She doesn't like her new job. | | |
| 3. She wants to give Ramón guitar lessons. | | |
| 4. She isn't good at sports. | | |
| 5. She is going to go out with Alberto. | | |

## 6. What do these people want? Complete the sentences. Choose the answers.

1. __b__ Emma wants Rebecca to __complete some forms__.
   a. sing a song    b. complete some forms

2. _____ Professor Thomas wants Rebecca to _____.
   a. take a test    b. work on her song

3. _____ Alex wants Rebecca to _____.
   a. give him guitar lessons    b. work in the restaurant

4. _____ Alberto wants Rebecca to _____.
   a. go out with him on Saturday    b. visit him at work

### What About YOU?

What do you think will happen? Check (✔) *I agree* or *I disagree*.

|   | I agree | I disagree |
|---|---|---|
| 1. Rebecca will teach guitar to Alex. | | |
| 2. Rebecca will have fun with Alberto. | | |

# WATCH FOR DETAILS

 **Watch PART 1.**

## WHILE You Watch

**7** What does Emma tell Rebecca to do? Check (✔) the sentences she says.

1. ✔ "You'll need to fill out these forms."
2. _____ "You'll have to say whether you're an American citizen."
3. _____ "You'll need to bring in some identification."
4. _____ "You'll need to bring in a résumé."
5. _____ "You'll need to be here at 2:30."

## AFTER You Watch

**8** How much do you remember about the story? Circle the answers.

1. (Rebecca)/Ramón needs to give information to Emma.
2. Rebecca/Ramón has a lot of homework.
3. Rebecca/Ramón takes Alex home.
4. Rebecca/Ramón wants to take the bus.
5. Rebecca/Ramón has a bad day.

**9** Check (✔) the sentences about Alex that are true.

1. ✔ He has a big spelling test tomorrow.
2. _____ He doesn't want Rebecca's help to study for his test.
3. _____ He wants Rebecca to take the bus home.
4. _____ He wants to take guitar lessons with Rebecca.
5. _____ He likes Rebecca.

**Watch PART 2.**

## WHILE You Watch

**10** Listen to Rebecca talk with her father. Circle the words she says.

1. "How is Kevin /(are you)?"
2. "My room out here is nice / small."
3. "The people in the house are very boring / interesting."
4. "Are you all right / tired?"
5. "School is a lot of work / easy."

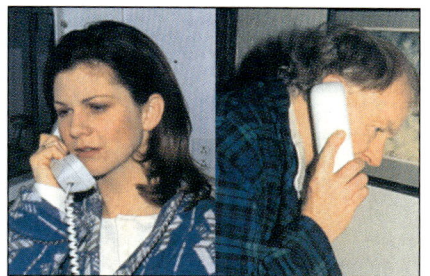

## AFTER You Watch

**11** How much do you remember about the story? Circle the answers.

1. Ramón /(Alberto) wants to see Rebecca on Saturday.
2. Mr. Casey is / isn't OK.
3. Rebecca says she is fine / sad in San Francisco.
4. Professor Thomas says Rebecca plays the guitar well / needs to practice the guitar.
5. Rebecca tells the children about a famous poem / song.

**12** What do you know about Rebecca's poem? Choose the answers.

1. _____ What is the poem called?
   a. "Traveling Blues"    b. "Take Me Out to the Ball Game"    c. "Casey at the Bat"
2. _____ What is the poem about?
   a. a policeman    b. a musician    c. a baseball player

 Check (✔) Yes or No.

|  | Yes | No |
|---|---|---|
| 1. Do you know any famous poems from your country? | _____ | _____ |
| 2. Are poems important to the culture of your country? | _____ | _____ |

EPISODE **17** page **5**

# Watch PART 3.

## WHILE You Watch

**13** Who is speaking? Write **R** for *Rebecca,* **E** for *Emma,* or **A** for *Alberto.*

1. __E__ "Congratulations. You're doing a splendid job."
2. _____ "How did you get so good at sports?"
3. _____ "So, are you free Saturday?"
4. _____ "What's the surprise?"
5. _____ "There's a gallery opening I'd love to take you to."

## AFTER You Watch

**14** How much do you remember about the story? Put the sentences in order from 1 to 5. Then write the sentences in the correct order below.

a. _____ Rebecca gets in Alberto's car.
b. _____ Ramón and Alex talk about guitar lessons.
c. _____ Alberto and Rebecca make a date.
d. _____ Emma and Ramón talk about Rebecca.
e. ___1___ Rebecca helps Alex play softball.

1. Rebecca helps Alex play softball.
2. _____
3. _____
4. _____
5. _____

**15** What are Alberto's plans for Saturday? Check (✔) the answers that are true.

1. _____ Go out with Rebecca.
2. _____ Go to an art gallery.
3. _____ Go to a baseball game.
4. _____ Pick up Rebecca at four o'clock.
5. _____ Have a Mexican dinner at Casa Mendoza.

 What sports do you play?

I _____.

# HIGHLIGHTS

## CULTURE

**In the United States and Canada, people use the titles "Mr.," "Mrs.," "Ms.," "Miss," and "Dr." to be formal. People use only first names to be informal.**

formal                informal

**What About YOU?**

1. What titles do people use in your country?
   They use _____.

2. What do these titles mean in English?
   They mean _____.

3. Are most people formal or informal when talking to others?
   Most people are _____.

## EXPRESSIONS

 **Match the underlined words from the story with their meanings.**

1. ___c___ Let's go
2. _____ What's it about?
3. _____ wearing nice clothes
4. _____ I'm sure

a.

b.

c.

d.

# REVIEW AND DISCUSS

## STORY SUMMARY

**17** Use the words in the box to complete the story summary for Episode 17.

| art | children | date | drives | father | fine | flowers | forms |
|---|---|---|---|---|---|---|---|
| good | ✓ job | note | questions | sick | talk | test | |

Emma gives Rebecca a ___job___(1). Then she asks Rebecca some _____(2) and gives her some _____(3) to fill out. Rebecca helps Alex study for a spelling _____(4). Then Ramón _____(5) Rebecca home. At home, Rebecca gets some _____(6) from Alberto. Alberto writes a _____(7) to Rebecca. He asks her to go out on a _____(8). Rebecca calls her _____(9). Mr. Casey says he is _____(10), but he is really _____(11). At work, Rebecca plays softball with the _____(12). Emma says Rebecca is doing a _____(13) job. Later, Ramón wants to _____(14) to Rebecca, but Rebecca is talking to Alberto. She and Alberto talk about an _____(15) gallery.

## VIEWPOINTS

**18** Watch the video discussion group. What does Roberto mean? Check (✓) *True* or *False*.

*Most men don't like to talk about their weaknesses.*

Roberto Arévalo, Colombia

|  | True | False |
|---|---|---|
| 1. Roberto is talking about Ramón. | _____ | _____ |
| 2. Roberto thinks Rebecca's father is sick. | _____ | _____ |

What is your opinion? Circle the answer.

What will happen to Rebecca's father?

a. He will be OK.    b. He will get very sick.    c. He will die.

# THE ART GALLERY

EPISODE 18

**PREVIEW** In this episode, the Mendoza family talks about the future. Rebecca goes on a date with Alberto.

*Why did you and Mom have to get divorced?*

Alex and Ramón at the ice cream parlor

*Alberto Mendoza! Your photos are part of the exhibit?*

Rebecca and Alberto at the art gallery

① *It's not only our business. It's our home.*
② *I disagree with Ramón.*

The Mendoza family at the restaurant

## BEFORE You Watch

**1** Look at the photos above. Complete the sentences. Choose the answers.

1. __a__ Alex is talking about his parents' __divorce__.
   a. divorce   b. jobs   c. house

2. _____ Rebecca and Alberto are in _____.
   a. a camera store   b. an art gallery   c. a restaurant

3. _____ Rebecca sees Alberto's _____.
   a. paintings   b. buildings   c. photos

4. _____ Ramón and Alberto are talking about _____.
   a. a photograph   b. the restaurant   c. a car

5. _____ Ramón and Alberto _____ about the restaurant.
   a. agree   b. disagree   c. laugh

What About YOU? What kind of art do you like?

I like _____.

…paintings   …photos

# WATCH FOR MAIN IDEAS

 Watch *all* of EPISODE 18, "The Art Gallery."

## WHILE You Watch

 **Where does Ramón go? Check (✔) all the answers.**

1. to an ice cream parlor ✔

2. to an art gallery ☐

3. to the restaurant ☐

4. to a family meeting ☐

## AFTER You Watch

 **How much do you remember about the story? Check (✔) the sentences that *are not* true.**

1. ___✔___ Mrs. Mendoza opens a letter.
2. _____ Ramón calls his ex-wife, Christine.
3. _____ Rebecca meets Alberto's friends at the art gallery.
4. _____ Rebecca sees Alberto's photographs.
5. _____ Ramón kisses Rebecca.
6. _____ The Mendoza family talks about the restaurant.
7. _____ Alberto takes Rebecca to a picnic.

**What happens? Circle the answers.**

1. (Alex)/Mrs. Mendoza asks Ramón if he will get married again.
2. Ramón/Christine is moving to Los Angeles.
3. Alex/Rebecca is surprised by Alberto's photographs.
4. Alberto/Ramón gives Rebecca a present.
5. Ramón/Alberto dances with his mother.

**What do these people want? Complete the sentences with the phrases below.**

a. to sell the restaurant
✔ d. to go to the picnic
b. to retire
e. to keep the restaurant
c. to take Alex to Los Angeles

1. _____ Christine wants _____.
2. _____ Ramón wants _____.
3. _____ Alberto wants _____.
4. __d__ Alex wants __to go to the picnic__.
5. _____ Mr. and Mrs. Mendoza want _____.

**How do these people feel? Complete the sentences. Choose the answers.**

1. _____ Ramón is _____ Christine.
   a. angry at   b. happy for
2. _____ Rebecca has a _____ with Alberto.
   a. good time   b. bad time
3. _____ Mr. and Mrs. Mendoza are _____ they want to sell the restaurant.
   a. sure   b. not sure

**What do you think will happen? Check (✔) Yes or No.**

|  | Yes | No |
|---|---|---|
| 1. Will Alex go to Los Angeles with his mother? | ____ | ____ |
| 2. Will Rebecca have time for school, work, *and* a boyfriend? | ____ | ____ |
| 3. Will the Mendoza family decide to sell the restaurant? | ____ | ____ |

# WATCH FOR DETAILS

 **Watch PART 1.**

## WHILE You Watch

**7** Who does Ramón talk to? Check (✔) their names.

1. Alex
   ✔

2. Mrs. Mendoza
   ☐

3. Rebecca
   ☐

4. Alberto
   ☐

## AFTER You Watch

**8** How much do you remember about the story? Check (✔) the sentences about Christine that are true.

1. ___✔___ She is Ramón's ex-wife.
2. _____ She is Alex's mother.
3. _____ She has a new husband.
4. _____ She is moving to New York.
5. _____ She wants Alex to live with her.

**9** How do these people feel? Use the words in the box to complete the sentences.

| angry | sad | tired | ✔ worried |

1. Alex is _____ about his parents' divorce.
2. Mrs. Mendoza is _____ and thinks about retiring.
3. Ramón is _____ about the letter from Christine.
4. Mrs. Mendoza is ___worried___ about Alex and Ramón.

 **What is your opinion?** Check (✔) *I agree* or *I disagree*.

|  | I agree | I disagree |
|---|---|---|
| 1. Ramón and Christine are friends. | _____ | _____ |
| 2. Alex should move to Los Angeles with his mother. | _____ | _____ |

## Watch PART 2.

### WHILE You Watch

**10** Watch Alberto and Rebecca in the gallery. Check (✔) the titles of Alberto's photographs.

1. __✔__ "Ramón and Alex"
2. _____ "Father and Son"
3. _____ "Rebecca"
4. _____ "Adventure Woman"
5. _____ "Dream Catcher"

### AFTER You Watch

**11** How much do you remember about the story? Check (✔) *True* or *False*.

|  | True | False |
|---|---|---|
| 1. Alberto's surprise is his photographs. | ✔ | ____ |
| 2. Rebecca doesn't like the photo of "Alex and Ramón." | ____ | ____ |
| 3. Rebecca is in the photo "Dream Catcher." | ____ | ____ |
| 4. Alberto doesn't want to see Rebecca again. | ____ | ____ |
| 5. Rebecca has homework to do. | ____ | ____ |

**12** What do you know about Rebecca and Alberto? Circle the answers.

1. Alberto (knows) / doesn't know a lot of people at the art gallery.
2. Rebecca is suprised / angry when she sees the photograph of herself.
3. Rebecca will see Alberto again next week / month.
4. Rebecca likes / doesn't like Alberto's gift.
5. The dream catcher lets the good / bad dreams through.

## Watch PART 3.

### WHILE You Watch

**13** Who is speaking? Write **M** for *Mr. Mendoza,* **A** for *Alberto,* or **R** for *Ramón.*

1. __M__ "Are you sure these investors are serious?"
2. _____ "They're very serious."
3. _____ "I don't think we should sell."
4. _____ "But why work so hard, Ramón?"
5. _____ "I like hard work."
6. _____ "Alberto, your mother and I need to discuss this some more."

### AFTER You Watch

**14** How much do you remember about the story? Check (✔) the sentences about the Casa Mendoza restaurant that are true.

1. __✔__ Some people want to buy it for a lot of money.
2. _____ It is the Mendozas' family business.
3. _____ It is a new restaurant.
4. _____ Ramón does not like to work there.
5. _____ Everybody in the Mendoza family wants to sell it.

**15** What do you know about the Mendoza family? Circle the answers.

1. Who is nervous about selling the restaurant?   (Mrs. Mendoza)/ Alex
2. Who wants to sell the restaurant?   Ramón / Alberto
3. Who will need money for Alex's education?   Ramón / Alberto
4. Who waits in the car?   Alex / Rebecca
5. Who is Alberto's note for?   Ramón / Rebecca

### What About YOU?

What is your opinion? Check (✔) *Yes* or *No*.

|  | Yes | No |
|---|---|---|
| 1. Is it a good idea to sell the restaurant? | _____ | _____ |
| 2. Is Alberto in love with Rebecca? | _____ | _____ |

# HIGHLIGHTS

## CULTURE

**In the United States and Canada, divorce is a difficult experience. It can also be very expensive. Many people...**

get a lawyer.

argue about the children.

  What is your opinion? Check (✔) *I agree* or *I disagree*.

|  | I agree | I disagree |
|---|---|---|
| 1. In my country many people are divorced. | _____ | _____ |
| 2. Divorce is OK. | _____ | _____ |
| 3. Divorce is difficult for children. | _____ | _____ |

## EXPRESSIONS

**16** Match the underlined words from the story with their meanings. Circle the answers.

1.

"Alberto is trying to <u>reach</u> you."
fight you / call you

2.

"I don't believe it. I knew something was <u>up</u>!"
happening / expensive

3.

"It makes me nervous, very nervous. Ramón, <u>speak up</u>."
stand up / say something

4.
"I'm always serious. I'm a serious <u>guy</u>."
man / brother

EPISODE **18** page **7**

# REVIEW AND DISCUSS

## STORY SUMMARY

**17** Use the words in the box to complete the story summary for Episode 18.

| art gallery | ✓ divorced | father | gives | keep | kisses | letter |
|---|---|---|---|---|---|---|
| Los Angeles | photographs | restaurant | sell | sure | takes | want |

Alex's parents are __divorced__ (1). Alex talks to his _____ (2) about it. Ramón gets a _____ (3) from Christine's lawyer. Christine and her husband are moving to _____ (4). They _____ (5) to take Alex with them. Alberto takes Rebecca to an _____ (6). Rebecca sees Alberto's _____ (7). One of the photographs is a picture of Rebecca. Alberto _____ (8) Rebecca home late. He _____ (9) her a dream catcher and _____ (10) her. The next day, the Mendoza family talks about the _____ (11). Alberto wants to _____ (12) the restaurant, Ramón wants to _____ (13) it, and Mr. and Mrs. Mendoza aren't _____ (14) about it.

## VIEWPOINTS

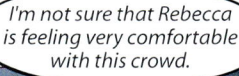

Nela Hosic, Bosnia

**18** Watch the video discussion group. What does Nela mean? Check (✓) *True* or *False*.

|  | True | False |
|---|---|---|
| 1. Nela is talking about the people at the art gallery. | _____ | _____ |
| 2. The gallery opening is a formal party. | _____ | _____ |

 **What About YOU?** What is your opinion? Check (✓) *Yes* or *No*.

|  | Yes | No |
|---|---|---|
| 1. Do you like formal parties? | _____ | _____ |
| 2. Do you like to wear formal clothes? | _____ | _____ |

# THE PICNIC

EPISODE 19

**PREVIEW** In this episode, Alex and Vincent go to a picnic. Some boys cause problems for Alex and Vincent.

Alex, Vincent, and Ramón at the race

Ramón and Rebecca in the park

Alex, Vincent, and the mean boys at the picnic

## BEFORE You Watch

**1** Look at the photos above. Check (✔) *True* or *False*.

|   | True | False |
|---|---|---|
| 1. Alex and Vincent win a race. | ✔ | |
| 2. Rebecca and Ramón talk about Alex. | ___ | ___ |
| 3. Rebecca wants Alex to go with his mother. | ___ | ___ |
| 4. Alex fights with a mean boy. | ___ | ___ |

**2** What do you know about Vincent? Check (✔) the answer that *is not* true.

_____ a. He wins a race.

_____ b. He has trouble with the mean boys.

_____ c. He doesn't go to the picnic.

**What About YOU?** What do you like to do at picnics?

I like to _____.

...play games   ...eat   ...talk to friends

# WATCH FOR MAIN IDEAS

 Watch *all* of EPISODE 19, "The Picnic."

## WHILE You Watch

 **What do the children do at the picnic? Check (✔) all the things you see.**

1. ____✔____ They run.
2. _____ They sing.
3. _____ They eat.
4. _____ They drink.
5. _____ They play.
6. _____ They dance.
7. _____ They fight.

## AFTER You Watch

 **How much do you remember about the story? Put the photos in order from 1 to 5.**

a. _____
b. _____
c. _____
d. _____
e. ____1____

**5** **What happens at the picnic? Complete the sentences. Choose the answers.**

1. __b__ Mr. Wang brings his ___wife___ to the picnic.
   a. sister    b. wife    c. daughter

2. _____ Ramón gives Rebecca _____ from Alberto.
   a. an invitation    b. a book    c. a kiss

3. _____ The boys call Vincent names because he _____.
   a. is Asian-American    b. wears glasses    c. is short

4. _____ The Wangs take Vincent _____.
   a. to the police    b. to the hospital    c. home

**6** **How do these people feel? Circle the answers.**

1. Vincent and Alex are
   a. happy    b. sad

2. The little boy is
   a. angry    b. hungry

3. Ramón and Rebecca are
   a. (tired)    b. unhappy

4. Mr. Wang is
   a. happy    b. angry

**What do you think will happen? Check (✔) Yes or No.**

|  | Yes | No |
|---|---|---|
| 1. Will Vincent come back to the picnic? | _____ | _____ |
| 2. Will Rebecca lose her job? | _____ | _____ |

EPISODE **19** page 3

# WATCH FOR DETAILS

 Watch PART 1.

## WHILE You Watch

 Who are these people? Circle their names.

1. Emma / Mrs. Wang

2. Emma / Mrs. Wang

3. Alex and Vincent / the mean boys

## AFTER You Watch

 How much do you remember about the story? Complete the sentences with the phrases below.

a. organizes a race
b. watch the picnic from the trees
c. are a team
d. introduces his wife to Rebecca
e. is learning English

1. ___d___ Mr. Wang _introduces his wife to Rebecca_.
2. _____ Mrs. Wang _____.
3. _____ Rebecca _____.
4. _____ Vincent and Alex _____.
5. _____ Two mean boys _____.

 What do you know about these people? Circle the answers.

1. Mrs. Wang's first name is (Mei-Lin)/ Susan.
2. Mr. Wang / Mrs. Wang wants to be a U.S. citizen.
3. Mr. and Mrs. Wang like / don't like Rebecca.
4. Vincent loves basketball / baseball.

EPISODE 19 page 4

## Watch PART 2.

## WHILE You Watch

**10** Who does Rebecca talk to? Check (✔) their names.

1. Alex
   ✔

2. the mean boys
   ☐

3. Emma
   ☐

4. Ramón
   ☐

## AFTER You Watch

**11** How much do you remember about the story? Circle the answers.

1. Who chases the mean boys?                       Rebecca / (Emma)
2. Who gets an invitation?                         Rebecca / Mrs. Wang
3. Who is having a retirement party?               Mr. and Mrs. Wang / Mr. and Mrs. Mendoza
4. Who wants to dance with Rebecca at the party?   Alex / Ramón
5. Who is divorced?                                Ramón / Rebecca

**12** Check (✔) the sentences about Alex that are true.

1. ___✔___ He is a good ball player.
2. _____ He knows that is mother is going to Los Angeles.
3. _____ His mother wants him to live in Los Angeles.
4. _____ His father wants him to live in Los Angeles.

 What is your opinion? Check (✔) *I agree* or *I disagree*.

|  | I agree | I disagree |
|---|---|---|
| 1. Ramón should tell Alex about Los Angeles. | _____ | _____ |
| 2. Alex will want to live in Los Angeles. | _____ | _____ |
| 3. Ramón and Rebecca are friends. | _____ | _____ |

EPISODE 19  page 5

Watch PART 3.

## WHILE You Watch

**13** Who is speaking? Write **A** for *Alex*, **R** for *Ramón*, or **W** for *Mr. Wang*.

1. __A__ "Hey, leave him alone!"
2. ____ "But these children were laughing at Vincent."
3. ____ "Come, Vincent, let's go home."
4. ____ "You should be ashamed of yourselves!"
5. ____ "I wanted to kill those kids."
6. ____ ". . . you should fight back with words, not with violence . . ."

## AFTER You Watch

**14** How much do you remember about the story? Put the sentences in order from 1 to 5. Then write the sentences in the correct order below.

a. _____ Rebecca and Ramón talk to the children.
b. _____ Alex fights with the mean boys.
c. _____ The Wangs go home.
d. ___1___ Two boys call Vincent racist names.
e. _____ Emma speaks to the Wangs.

1. __Two boys call Vincent racist names.__
2. _____
3. _____
4. _____
5. _____

**What About YOU?** What do you do when you are angry at someone?

I _____.

…walk away   …use words   …fight

# HIGHLIGHTS

## CULTURE

**When a person doesn't like a group of people because they have a different skin color or are from a different country, it is called racism. In the United States, Canada, and other countries, people fight racism in many ways. Some ways are . . .**

education in school.

education at home.

laws.

**What about your country? Check (✔) *True* or *False*.**

|  | True | False |
|---|---|---|
| 1. There is no racism in my country. | _____ | _____ |
| 2. People talk about racism in the schools. | _____ | _____ |
| 3. There are laws against racism. | _____ | _____ |

## EXPRESSIONS

 **Match the underlined words from the story with their meanings.**

1. _____ Watch
2. ___c___ What's happening?
3. _____ Leave!
4. _____ stop

a.

b.

c.

d.

# STORY SUMMARY

**16** Use the words in the box to complete the story summary for Episode 19.

| angry | boys | children | food | hits | leave |
|---|---|---|---|---|---|
| ✔ picnic | race | runs | take | tells | winners |

Mr. Wang, Mrs. Wang, and Vincent arrive at the ___picnic___ (1). Rebecca starts a _____ (2). Vincent and Alex are the _____ (3). Later, two boys take _____ (4) from the picnic. Emma _____ (5) after them. Ramón _____ (6) Rebecca about his divorce. Ramón doesn't want his ex-wife to _____ (7) Alex to Los Angeles. Then the two _____ (8) call Vincent racist names and push him. Alex _____ (9) one of the boys. Vincent and the Wangs _____ (10) the picnic because some of the _____ (11) laugh at Vincent. Ramón and Rebecca are _____ (12) at the children.

# VIEWPOINTS

**17** Watch the video discussion group. What does Hai mean? Complete the sentences. Choose the answers.

1. _____ Hai is explaining how _____ feels.
   a. Mr. Wang    b. Ramón

2. _____ Hai thinks Mr. Wang should _____.
   a. take Vincent home    b. try to talk about the problem

*It's a human reaction to protect and to avoid confrontation.... but you will need to face the situation.*

Hai B. Pho, Vietnam

## What About YOU?

What is your opinion? Check (✔) *I agree* or *I disagree*.

|  | I agree | I disagree |
|---|---|---|
| 1. It is a good idea for the Wangs to leave. | _____ | _____ |
| 2. Emma and Rebecca feel bad about the fight. | _____ | _____ |

# PREJUDICE

EPISODE 20

**PREVIEW** In this episode, the children talk to a police officer. They make cards for Vincent. Vincent talks with his mother.

① *Let's talk about what happened. Who wants to start?*
② *Some boys started calling Vincent names.*

Emma, Officer Jones, and the children at the after-school program

*Class, listen to this wonderful card: "To Vincent, you are my friend." Isn't that nice?*

Emma and the children at the after-school program

*Mom, why can't I go back to the after-school program? I miss my friends.*

Vincent and Mrs. Wang at home

## BEFORE You Watch

**1** Look at the photos above. Circle the answers.

1. The children are at  a picnic / <u>the after-school program</u>.
2. Officer Jones wants to  <u>help / yell at</u>  the children.
3. The children talk about the  <u>race / mean boys</u>.
4. The children  <u>sing a song / write letters</u>  to Vincent.
5. Vincent  <u>wants / doesn't want</u>  to go back to the after-school program.
6. Vincent wants to see his  <u>friends / father</u>.

What do you do when you're sorry for something?

I _____.

…send a card  …call my friend  …visit my friend

# WATCH FOR MAIN IDEAS

 Watch *all* of EPISODE 20, "Prejudice."

## WHILE You Watch

**2** Who talks to the children? Check (✔) their names.

  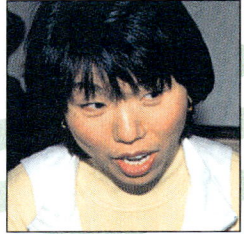 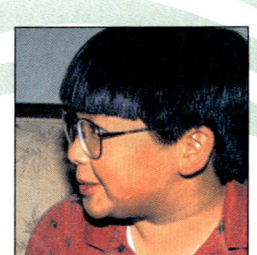 

1. Emma ✔
2. Officer Jones ☐
3. Mrs. Wang ☐
4. Vincent ☐
5. Rebecca ☐

## AFTER You Watch

**3** How much do you remember about the story? Circle the answers.

1. Officer Jones comes to the Wangs' house / (after-school program).
2. Officer Jones talks about the mean boys / police.
3. Emma wants the children to write letters / call Vincent.
4. Vincent is at the after-school program / home.
5. The children write nice / mean letters.

**4** What does Officer Jones say about hate crimes? Check (✔) the answer that is true.

Hate crimes. . .

_____ a. are sometimes OK.

_____ b. are about someone's race or religion.

_____ c. only happen to children.

**5** What do you know about these people? Use the names in the box to complete the sentences.

| ✔ The children | Emma | A police officer | Rebecca | Vincent |

1. _____ visits the after-school program.
2. _The children_ laughed at Vincent.
3. _____ wants to go back to the after-school program.
4. _____ asks the children to write letters to Vincent.
5. _____ talks with Alex about Vincent's card.

**6** What do the children want Vincent to do? Circle the answer.

a. ...fight the mean boys
b. ...stay home
c. ...return to the after-school program

 What do you think will happen? Check (✔) Yes or No.

|  | Yes | No |
|---|---|---|
| 1. Will Vincent go to the after-school program again? | _____ | _____ |
| 2. Will the police find the two boys? | _____ | _____ |
| 3. Will Vincent like his friends' cards? | _____ | _____ |

# WATCH FOR DETAILS

**Watch PART 1.**

## WHILE You Watch

**7** Listen to the children talk about the picnic. Check (✔) the things they say.

1. __✔__ "Some boys started calling Vincent names."
2. _____ "They took some food."
3. _____ "We ate a lot of food."
4. _____ "There was a fight."
5. _____ "We liked the picnic."
6. _____ "A crime?"

## AFTER You Watch

**8** How much do you remember about the story? Check (✔) *True* or *False*.

|   | True | False |
|---|---|---|
| 1. Emma wants to talk about Vincent and the picnic. | ✔ | ____ |
| 2. Officer Jones asks the children some questions. | ____ | ____ |
| 3. The children feel good about the picnic. | ____ | ____ |
| 4. Officer Jones is angry at Vincent. | ____ | ____ |
| 5. The children learn from Officer Jones. | ____ | ____ |

**9** What do you know about these people? Complete the sentences with the phrases below.

a. is Asian-American
✔ c. tell Officer Jones about the picnic
b. was angry at the mean boys
d. teaches children about hate crimes

1. __c__ The children __tell Officer Jones about the picnic__.
2. ____ Officer Jones _____.
3. ____ Alex _____.
4. ____ The two boys were mean to Vincent because he _____.

### What About YOU?

What is your opinion? Check (✔) *I agree* or *I disagree*.

|   | I agree | I disagree |
|---|---|---|
| 1. Officer Jones is nice to the children. | ____ | ____ |
| 2. The children are really sorry about Vincent. | ____ | ____ |

**Watch PART 2.**

## WHILE You Watch

**10** What does Emma tell the children? Circle the words she says.

1. "Now, what happened is called a crime / prejudice."
2. "But guess what? We're all different / the same."
3. "I must be wrong / confused."
4. "Oh, you two are the same, you're brothers / sisters, aren't you?"
5. "That's when it became our problem / picnic."

## AFTER You Watch

**11** How much do you remember about the story? Put the sentences in order from 1 to 5. Then write the sentences in the correct order below.

a. _____ Emma says the children all look alike.
b. _____ Emma and the children decide to write letters to Vincent.
c. _____ The children say prejudice does not feel good.
d. __1__ Emma talks about prejudice.
e. _____ The children say they aren't alike.

1. Emma talks about prejudice.
2. _____
3. _____
4. _____
5. _____

**12** What does Emma think? Check (✔) all the answers.

1. __✔__ Prejudice is bad.
2. _____ Alex and Vincent look alike.
3. _____ Everyone is different.
4. _____ Vincent's parents want Vincent to come back to the after-school program.
5. _____ The children need to write letters to Vincent.

## Watch PART 3.

## WHILE You Watch

**13** Who is speaking? Write **A** for *Alex*, **E** for *Emma*, or **V** for *Vincent*.

1. __V__ "Alex didn't laugh at me."
2. ____ "Please let me go back, Mommy."
3. ____ "Why did you laugh?"
4. ____ "You don't think it's funny now, do you?"
5. ____ "Vincent, you have to come back."

## AFTER You Watch

**14** How much do you remember about the story? Complete the sentences. Choose the answers.

1. __a__ Mrs. Wang practices __English__.
   a. English   b. Chinese   c. baseball

2. _____ Vincent wants to _____.
   a. read a book   b. watch TV   c. go back to the after-school program

3. _____ The _____ make cards for Vincent.
   a. police   b. teachers   c. children

4. _____ Alex misses _____.
   a. Vincent   b. Emma   c. Rebecca

**15** What do you know about Vincent and his mother? Complete the sentences with *Vincent* or *Mrs. Wang*.

1. __Mrs. Wang__ doesn't speak English well.
2. _____ wants to see his friends.
3. _____ thinks the children at the after-school program aren't nice.
4. _____ says Alex didn't laugh.

What is your opinion? Check (✔) *True* or *False*.

|  | True | False |
|---|---|---|
| 1. Vincent is sad. | _____ | _____ |
| 2. Vincent is angry at his mother. | _____ | _____ |

# HIGHLIGHTS

## CULTURE

**In the United States and Canada, police officers work with the people in their communities to make life safer for everyone. For example, they . . .**

talk to children.

talk to people in neighborhoods.

help stop crime in neighborhoods.

**What happens in your country? Check (✔) Yes or No.**

|  | Yes | No |
|---|---|---|
| 1. Do the police work with the people in their communities? | _____ | _____ |
| 2. Do the police talk to children in schools? | _____ | _____ |

## EXPRESSIONS

 **Match the underlined words from the story with their meanings.**

1. _____ are wearing
2. _____ return
3. _____ tell him
4. ____a____ Do you know something?

a.

b.

c.

d.

# REVIEW AND DISCUSS

## STORY SUMMARY

**17** Use the words in the box to complete the story summary for Episode 20.

| asks | cards | children | ✔ comes | English |
|------|-------|----------|---------|---------|
| friends | help | mother | prejudice | program | want | write |

A police officer __comes__ (1) to the after-school program. She talks to the _____ (2) about hate crimes. Emma talks about _____ (3) and _____ (4) the children to make _____ (5). At home, Vincent helps his _____ (6) with her _____ (7) lesson. He wants to return to the _____ (8) and see his _____ (9). The children _____ (10) their letters. Emma and Rebecca _____ (11) them. The children _____ (12) Vincent to come back.

## VIEWPOINTS

*She said, "Of course we accept checks." Then she looked up and saw me, and she said, "No."*

Emma

**18** Watch the Reflections segment. Choose the answers.

1. _____ Why doesn't the store clerk take Emma's check?
   a. Emma is different from the clerk.
   b. Emma doesn't have any money.

2. _____ How does Emma feel when this happens?
   a. She is unhappy.
   b. She doesn't care.

What can we do to end prejudice?

We can _____.

*...teach respect*

*...be a good example to others*

# A DIFFICULT DECISION

**EPISODE 21**

**PREVIEW** In this episode, the Wangs make a decision about Vincent and the after-school program.

Emma, Rebecca, and Mr. Wang at the store

Vincent, Mrs. Wang, and Emma at the after-school program

Rebecca, Alex, and Ramón at the after-school program

## BEFORE You Watch

**1** Look at the photos above. Complete the sentences. Choose the answers.

1. __a__ Emma and Rebecca see Mr. Wang at the ___Wangs' store___.
   a. Wangs' store    b. Wangs' home    c. bus station

2. _____ The Wang family decides about _____.
   a. money    b. music school    c. Vincent and the after-school program

3. _____ Vincent _____ come back to the after-school program.
   a. can    b. will    c. won't

4. _____ Emma _____ about the Wangs' decision.
   a. is happy    b. is sad    c. doesn't know

5. _____ Rebecca wants to talk to the Wangs about _____.
   a. piano lessons    b. guitar lessons    c. English lessons

**What About YOU?** What is your opinion? Check (✓) *I agree* or *I disagree*.

|  | I agree | I disagree |
|---|---|---|
| 1. Sometimes I make difficult decisions. | _____ | _____ |
| 2. Everyone always agrees with me. | _____ | _____ |

EPISODE 21 page 1

# WATCH FOR MAIN IDEAS

 Watch *all* of EPISODE 21, "A Difficult Decision."

## WHILE You Watch

 Where does Rebecca go? Check (✔) all the answers.

**1.** the Wangs' store
✔

**2.** the after-school program
☐

**3.** Emma's office
☐

**4.** the San Francisco College of Music
☐

**5.** the Wangs' home
☐

## AFTER You Watch

 How much do you remember about the story? Use the words in the box to complete the sentences.

| ✔ cards | Emma | guitar | home | studies | Vincent |

**1.** Emma and Rebecca bring the children's ____cards____ to Mr. Wang.

**2.** Mr. Wang gives the cards to _____.

**3.** Rebecca _____ hard at music school.

**4.** Mrs. Wang talks to _____ about Vincent and the after-school program.

**5.** Rebecca wants to give _____ lessons to Vincent and Alex.

**6.** Rebecca goes to the Wangs' _____ to talk to Mrs. Wang.

**4** What do you know about these people? Check (✔) *True* or *False*.

|  | True | False |
|---|---|---|
| 1. Rebecca and Emma hope Alex returns to the program. | ✔ | ___ |
| 2. Mr. Wang says the family's decision is easy. | ___ | ___ |
| 3. Vincent likes the cards from his friends. | ___ | ___ |
| 4. Alex is happy about the Wangs' decision. | ___ | ___ |
| 5. Rebecca has an idea for Vincent and Alex. | ___ | ___ |

 **5** What is Rebecca's idea? Check (✔) the answer.

Write a letter to Vincent.

a. _____

Take Alex and Vincent to a movie.

b. _____

Play a baseball game.

c. _____

Teach Alex and Vincent how to play the guitar.

d. _____

 What do you think will happen? Check (✔) *Yes* or *No*.

|  | Yes | No |
|---|---|---|
| 1. Will Mrs. Wang let Vincent take guitar lessons? | ___ | ___ |
| 2. Will Vincent be happy about the guitar lessons? | ___ | ___ |

# WATCH FOR DETAILS

 **Watch PART 1.**

## WHILE You Watch

 Who talks to Mr. Wang about the after-school program? Check (✓) their names.

1. ___✓___ Emma
2. _____ Rebecca
3. _____ Alex
4. _____ Vincent
5. _____ Ramón

## AFTER You Watch

 How much do you remember about the story? Put the photos in order from 1 to 5.

a. _____

b. _____

c. _____

d. ___1___

e. _____

a. Mrs. Washington and Miss Casey brought these for you.

b. Parents must protect their children.

c. ① Dad, can't I go back? ② We'll see.

d. ① He's not ready to change his mind. ② He knows Vincent loved the program.

e. The children from the after-school program made these cards for Vincent.

 Why does Emma want Vincent to come back to the program? Check (✓) the answers that are true.

1. ___✓___ She and Rebecca are sorry.
2. _____ The people at the program miss Vincent.
3. _____ She wants Vincent to be friends with the mean boys.
4. _____ The police have the two mean boys.
5. _____ She wants Mr. Wang to help her fight prejudice.

## Watch PART 2.

### WHILE You Watch

**9** Who is speaking? Write **R** for *Rebecca*, **E** for *Emma*, or **V** for *Vincent*.

1. __R__ "Do you think Vincent's coming back?"
2. _____ "Vincent! Mrs. Wang! Come in!"
3. _____ "We'll miss you very much."
4. _____ "It was nice here. I liked it a lot."
5. _____ "…my mother says we have to go now."
6. _____ "Alex, I have some bad news…."

### AFTER You Watch

**10** How much do you remember about the story? Circle the answers.

1. Vincent and Mrs. Wang see Emma at   home / the after-school program.
2. Vincent and Mrs. Wang give Emma the   cards / guitar.
3. Emma (likes) / doesn't like Vincent.
4. Vincent likes / doesn't like the after-school program.
5. Emma is sorry / happy that Vincent won't come back.
6. Rebecca tells / doesn't tell Alex about Vincent.

**What About YOU?** What is your opinion? Check (✔) *True* or *False*.

|  | True | False |
|---|---|---|
| 1. The Wangs' decision is difficult. | _____ | _____ |
| 2. Vincent helps make the decision. | _____ | _____ |
| 3. Alex is happy about the decision. | _____ | _____ |

## Watch PART 3.

### WHILE You Watch

**11** Listen to Ramón talk to Rebecca. Circle the words he says.

1. "How was your day / school?"
2. "That's too nice / bad."
3. "What do you think / know, Alex?"
4. "But I must pay for Alex's / Vincent's lessons."
5. "Listen, Vincent is Alex's favorite / best friend."

### AFTER You Watch

**12** How much do you remember about the story? Circle the answers.

1. Who picks Alex up at the program?      (Ramón) / Mr. Wang
2. Who tells Ramón about the Wangs' decision?   Alex / Rebecca
3. Who wants to pay for Alex's guitar lessons?   Emma / Ramón
4. Who wants to start the lessons today?    Alex / Ramón
5. Who goes to the Wangs' house?     Rebecca / Ramón

**13** Why does Rebecca want to give guitar lessons to Alex and Vincent? Check (✔) the answers that are true.

1. ___✔___ She wants Alex and Vincent to be together.
2. _____ She wants Alex and Vincent to play the guitar.
3. _____ She needs the money.
4. _____ She is sorry about the picnic.

### What About YOU?

What is your opinion? Check (✔) *I agree* or *I disagree*.

|   | I agree | I disagree |
|---|---------|------------|
| 1. Rebecca should give free guitar lessons to the boys. | _____ | _____ |
| 2. Mrs. Wang will like Rebecca's idea. | _____ | _____ |

# HIGHLIGHTS

## CULTURE

In the United States, Canada, and around the world, people use computers for more and more things.

For example, Bill uses a computer to write music. Other people use them to learn English, and to write and send mail.

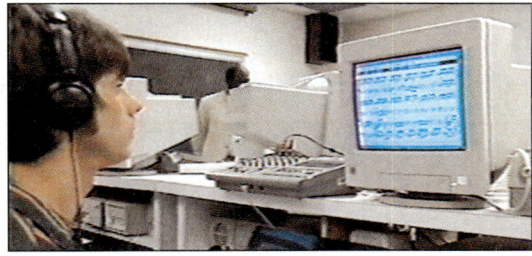

Do you use a computer?
What do you use it for?

I use a computer to _____.

## EXPRESSIONS

 **Match the underlined words from the story with their meanings.**

1. ___c___ ". . . let's keep our fingers crossed."

2. _____ "Have a seat, please."

3. _____ "That's too bad."

4. _____ "Take it easy!"

a.

b.

c.

d.

# REVIEW AND DISCUSS

## STORY SUMMARY

**15** Use the words in the box to complete the story summary for Episode 21.

| cards | day | difficult | gives | guitar | idea |
| isn't | likes | program | sad | talk | ✔ visit | wants |

Emma and Rebecca __**visit**__(1) Mr. Wang. They bring him the children's _____(2). They want Vincent to come back to the _____(3). It is a _____(4) decision for the Wangs. Mr. Wang _____(5) the cards to Vincent. Vincent _____(6) them. He _____(7) to return to the program. The next _____(8), Mrs. Wang and Vincent talk to Emma at the after-school program. Vincent _____(9) going to come back. Alex is _____(10). Rebecca has an _____(11). She wants to give _____(12) lessons to Vincent and Alex. Alex and Vincent like the idea. Rebecca needs to _____(13) to the Wangs about it.

## VIEWPOINTS

**16** Watch the video discussion group. What does Roberto mean? Complete the sentences. Choose the answers.

1. _____ Roberto is talking about _____.

    a. Ramón and Alex    b. the Wangs

2. _____ Roberto _____ with the Wangs' decision.

    a. agrees    b. disagrees

*I don't think it's a very good decision, but that's what they decide to do because they're hurt.*

**Roberto Arévalo, Colombia**

### What About YOU?

What is your opinion? Check (✔) Yes or No.

|  | Yes | No |
|---|---|---|
| 1. Do the Wangs make the right decision? | _____ | _____ |
| 2. Is Mr. Wang a mean person? | _____ | _____ |

# GUITAR LESSONS

**PREVIEW** In this episode, Rebecca talks to the Wangs about guitar lessons. Rebecca also learns more about Ramón, his ex-wife, and Alex.

Vincent, Mrs. Wang, and Rebecca at the Wangs' house

Ramón and his mother at home

Ramón and Rebecca at the after-school program

## BEFORE You Watch

**1** Look at the photos above. Check (✔) *True* or *False*.

|  | True | False |
|---|---|---|
| 1. Rebecca talks to Mrs. Wang. | ✔ | |
| 2. Vincent doesn't want guitar lessons. | | |
| 3. Rebecca says that the lessons are $20.00. | | |
| 4. Ramón goes to see Christine. | | |
| 5. Ramón feels bad about his talk with Alex's mother. | | |
| 6. Rebecca isn't worried about Ramón. | | |

What instrument do you play?

I _____.

…play the guitar   …don't play an instrument   …play the piano

EPISODE 22  page 1

# WATCH FOR MAIN IDEAS

 Watch *all* of EPISODE 22, "Guitar Lessons."

## WHILE You Watch

 **Where are these people? Circle the answers.**

1. **at the Wangs' house** / at the after-school program

2. at the restaurant / at the Mendozas' house

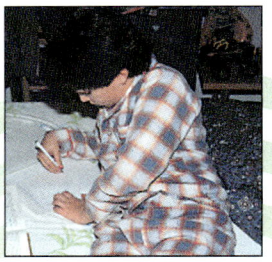

3. at the Mendozas' house / at a hotel

4. at the music school / at the after-school program

## AFTER You Watch

 **How much do you remember about the story? Put the photos in order from 1 to 5.**

a. _____
b. __1__
c. _____
d. _____
e. _____

a. *You're not going to let her take Alex to Los Angeles, are you?*

b. *This is very kind of you…but why?*

c. *I don't know what I'm going to tell Alex.*

d. *Are you and Miss Casey going to date?*

e. ① *I know somebody he likes.* ② *Who's that?*

**4** Who are these sentences about? Use the words in the box to complete the sentences.

> ✔ Alex    Ramón    Rebecca    Vincent    Mrs. Wang

1. His mother wants to take ____Alex____ to Los Angeles.
2. _____ wants Alex to live with him in San Francisco.
3. _____ gives Rebecca a present.
4. _____ will take guitar lessons with Alex.
5. _____ will give guitar lessons to Vincent and Alex.

**5** What do you know about these people? Check (✔) *True* or *False*.

|   | True | False |
|---|---|---|
| 1. Vincent and Alex are happy about the guitar lessons. | ✔ | _____ |
| 2. Ramón and Christine are married. | _____ | _____ |
| 3. Mrs. Mendoza doesn't want Alex to clean the floor. | _____ | _____ |
| 4. Alex is reading a science book. | _____ | _____ |
| 5. Ramón and Rebecca talk about Alex's mother. | _____ | _____ |

**6** What does Mrs. Mendoza think? Check (✔) the sentence that *is not* true.

_____ a. Ramón needs a wife.

_____ b. Alex should go to Los Angeles.

_____ c. Alex watches a lot of TV.

**What About YOU?** What do you think will happen? Check (✔) *Yes* or *No*.

|   | Yes | No |
|---|---|---|
| 1. Will Vincent and Alex like the guitar lessons? | _____ | _____ |
| 2. Will Alex go to live in Los Angeles with his mother? | _____ | _____ |

# WATCH FOR DETAILS

 Watch PART 1.

## WHILE You Watch

 **Listen to Vincent and Alex's phone conversation. Circle the words they say.**

1. Vincent: "My (mom)/ dad says we can do it."
2. Alex: "Cool. Where / When ?"
3. Vincent: "Starting next Saturday / Tuesday, after the program."
4. Alex: "Good / Great !"
5. Vincent: "Hey, tell everybody the books / cards were great."

## AFTER You Watch

 **How much do you remember about the story? Circle the answers.**

1. Rebecca wants /(doesn't want) money for the guitar lessons.
2. Mrs. Wang calls Mr. Wang / Ramón to talk about the lessons.
3. Mr. Wang is happy / unhappy about guitar lessons.
4. Mrs. Wang wants / doesn't want to pay.
5. Mrs. Wang gives / doesn't give a present to Rebecca.
6. The guitar lessons will be at the after-school program / Wangs' house.

**Check (✔) the sentences about Rebecca that are true.**

1. ___✔___ She feels bad about what happened to Vincent at the picnic.
2. _____ She goes to the Wangs' house with Ramón.
3. _____ She will bring Alex to the guitar lessons.
4. _____ Mrs. Wang doesn't like her.
5. _____ She doesn't like Mrs. Wang's present.
6. _____ Alex and Vincent are important to her.

EPISODE 22 page 4

**Watch PART 2.**

## WHILE You Watch

**10** Which parts of the Mendozas' house do you see? Check (✔) all the answers.

1. the kitchen ✔

2. the family room ☐

3. the bathroom ☐

4. the basement ☐

5. Alex's bedroom ☐

## AFTER You Watch

**11** How much do you remember about the story? Put the sentences in order from 1 to 5.

a. _____ Ramón goes to see Christine.

b. __1__ Alex asks Ramón about Miss Casey.

c. _____ Ramón talks to his mother in the basement.

d. _____ Alex spills popcorn on the floor.

e. _____ Ramón tells Alex to do his homework.

 What is your opinion? Check (✔) *I agree* or *I disagree*.

|   | I agree | I disagree |
|---|---|---|
| 1. Mrs. Mendoza wants Ramón to get married again. | _____ | _____ |
| 2. Alex wants his father to get married again. | _____ | _____ |
| 3. Ramón wants to get married again. | _____ | _____ |

Watch PART 3.

## WHILE You Watch

**12** Who is speaking? Write *A* for *Alex*, *M* for *Mrs. Mendoza*, or *R* for *Ramón*.

1. __M__ "What are you studying?"
2. ____ "Is Daddy going to get married again?"
3. ____ "I don't know."
4. ____ "I know somebody he likes."
5. ____ "She's moving to L.A."
6. ____ "I want him to stay here."

## AFTER You Watch

**13** How much do you remember about the story? Complete the sentences with the phrases below.

  a. is moving to Los Angeles
✔ b. thinks Ramón likes Rebecca
  c. listens to Ramón's problems
  d. talks to Alex about science and his parents
  e. fights with Christine about Alex

1. __b__ Alex __thinks Ramón likes Rebecca_____.
2. _____ Mrs. Mendoza _____.
3. _____ Ramón _____.
4. _____ Rebecca _____.
5. _____ Christine _____.

What do you think will happen? Check (✔) *Yes* or *No*.

|  | Yes | No |
|---|---|---|
| 1. Will Ramón tell Alex about Los Angeles? | ____ | ____ |
| 2. Will a judge decide where Alex lives? | ____ | ____ |

# HIGHLIGHTS

## CULTURE

**Watching television is a very popular activity in the United States and Canada.**

How important is television in your country and in your house?
Check (✓) *True* or *False*.

|  | True | False |
|---|---|---|
| 1. Television is popular in my country. | _____ | _____ |
| 2. I watch more than 3 hours of TV each day. | _____ | _____ |
| 3. I watch less than 1 hour of TV each day. | _____ | _____ |

*Source: U.S. Bureau of the Census, *Statistical Abstract of the United States*, 1996; Ministry of Industry, Science and Technology of Canada, *Statistics Canada*, 1994. The totals above are national averages, and include the viewing of network TV, cable TV, and home video cassettes.

## EXPRESSIONS

 **Match the underlined words from the story with their meanings. Circle the answers.**

1. (return very soon) / make dinner

2. bad / great

3. teaching / dating

4. look at / do

# REVIEW AND DISCUSS

## STORY SUMMARY

**15** Use the words in the box to complete the story summary for Episode 22.

| agree | happy | home | lessons | like | live |
| sees | talk | thinks | ✔ visits | worried | |

Rebecca __visits__(1) Vincent and Mrs. Wang. They talk about guitar _____(2) for Vincent and Alex. The Wangs _____(3) Rebecca's idea. Alex and Vincent are _____(4). At _____(5), Mrs. Mendoza talks to Ramón and Alex. Alex _____(6) Ramón likes Rebecca. Later, Ramón _____(7) his ex-wife, Christine. They don't _____(8) about where Alex should _____(9). Ramón tells Rebecca about his _____(10) with Christine. He is _____(11) about Alex's future.

## VIEWPOINTS

**16** Watch the video discussion group. What does Hai mean? Check (✔) *True* or *False*.

*I really think the father should have custody of the son.*

Hai B. Pho,
Vietnam

|  | True | False |
|---|---|---|
| 1. Hai is talking about Vincent and Mr. Wang. | ____ | ____ |
| 2. Hai thinks Alex should stay with Ramón. | ____ | ____ |

**What About YOU?** What is your opinion? Check (✔) *I agree* or *I disagree*.

|  | I agree | I disagree |
|---|---|---|
| 1. Alex should stay with his father. | ____ | ____ |
| 2. Alex should go with his mother. | ____ | ____ |
| 3. Ramón and Christine should talk to a judge. | ____ | ____ |

# THE RETIREMENT PARTY

**PREVIEW** In this episode, Ramón and Alex talk about Alex's mother. The Mendozas have their retirement party.

*So, your mom wants you to move, and I want you to stay.*

Alex and Ramón at home

*Rebecca's studying music, and she's going to be a songwriter someday.*

Alberto, Rebecca, and friends at the party

① *No, they're just friends. She's Alex's teacher. That's all.*
② *Don't be too sure.*

Mrs. Mendoza and Alice at the party

## BEFORE You Watch

**1** Look at the photos above. Complete the sentences with words below.

   a. Rebecca
   b. his mother's plans
   ✔ c. bedroom
   d. retirement party

1. __c__ Alex and Ramón are in Alex's __bedroom__.

2. _____ Ramón tells Alex about _____.

3. _____ Alberto and Rebecca are at the _____.

4. _____ Mrs. Mendoza and Alice Goodman talk about Ramón and _____.

What is your opinion? Check (✔) *I agree* or *I disagree*.

|  | I agree | I disagree |
|---|---|---|
| Alex understands his parents' feelings. | _____ | _____ |

# WATCH FOR MAIN IDEAS

Watch *all* of EPISODE 23, "The Retirement Party."

## WHILE You Watch

 What places do you see in this episode? Check (✔) all the answers.

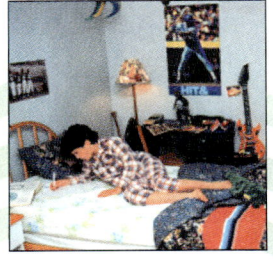

1. the Mendozas' house ✔

2. the music school ☐

3. the after-school program ☐

4. Nancy's house ☐

5. the restaurant ☐

## AFTER You Watch

 How much do you remember about the story? Put the sentences in order from 1 to 8.

At the Mendozas' house...

a. _____ Ramón and Alex talk about Los Angeles in Alex's bedroom.

b. _____ Alex gets angry and leaves the bedroom.

c. ___1___ Ramón and Alex talk in the kitchen.

At the party...

d. _____ Alberto and Rebecca enter the restaurant.

e. _____ Rebecca meets Alice Goodman.

f. _____ Mr. and Mrs. Mendoza dance.

g. _____ Alice and Mrs. Mendoza talk about Ramón and Rebecca.

h. _____ Rebecca meets Gloria Díaz.

**4** **What do you know about these people? Circle the answers.**

1. Alex is  surprised / not surprised  that his mother is moving.
2. In the afternoon, Rebecca  goes out with Alberto / studies at school .
3. Rebecca goes to the party with  Ramón / Alberto .
4. Gloria Díaz knows  Alberto / Alex .
5. Alice Goodman is  Mrs. Mendoza's / Rebecca's  friend.
6. Alice asks Mrs. Mendoza about Alberto's  job / girlfriends .

**5** **What does Alex want? Circle the answer.**

a. ...to go to Los Angeles
b. ...to have his parents together again
c. ...to dance with Rebecca

**What About YOU?** **What do you think will happen? Check (✔) Yes or No.**

|  | Yes | No |
|---|---|---|
| 1. Alex, his mother, and his father will be a family again. | _____ | _____ |
| 2. Alberto will go on a date with Gloria Díaz. | _____ | _____ |

# WATCH FOR DETAILS

 **Watch PART 1.**

## WHILE You Watch

**6** **What does Ramón tell Alex? Circle the words he says.**

1. "I talked to your friend / (mother) last night."
2. "She and Norman want to talk to me / you about something important."
3. "Norman got a new job / house in Los Angeles."
4. "They're moving to / visiting Los Angeles."
5. "The end of the week / month."

## AFTER You Watch

**7** **How much do you remember about the story? Complete the conversations with the sentences below.**

✔ a. Well, she and Norman want you to move to L.A. with them.
   b. I don't think that's possible.
   c. Out!
   d. At the end of the month.

1. _____
2. __a__
3. _____
4. _____

 **What is your opinion? Check (✔) Yes or No.**

|  | Yes | No |
|---|---|---|
| 1. Is Alex angry at his parents? | _____ | _____ |
| 2. Does Alex understand their divorce? | _____ | _____ |

EPISODE 23 page 4

## Watch PART 2.

### WHILE You Watch

**8** Listen to Rebecca's conversation with Bill. Check (✔) the sentences she says.

_____ 1. "I'm going to a big party tonight."

_____ 2. "Can you get me an invitation?"

_____ 3. "Forget it!"

✔ 4. "They're really nice people."

_____ 5. "See you!"

### AFTER You Watch

**9** How much do you remember about the story? Circle the answers.

1. Bill wants / (doesn't want) to go to the retirement party with Rebecca.
2. "Old people" make Bill happy / nervous.
3. Rebecca meets Gloria Díaz / Mrs. Mendoza for the first time.
4. Rebecca and Alberto tell Gloria about the art gallery / desert.
5. Gloria talks about her trip to Acapulco in English / Spanish.
6. Rebecca understands / doesn't understand Gloria's story.

**10** What do you know about Alberto? Check (✔) the sentences that *are not* true.

_____ a. Alberto knows Gloria.

✔ b. Alberto doesn't like Gloria.

_____ c. Alberto understands Spanish.

_____ d. Alberto wants to move to Los Angeles.

## Watch PART 3.

## WHILE You Watch

**11** Who is speaking? Write **A** for *Alice*, or **M** for *Mrs. Mendoza*.

1. __A__ "Retirement can get a little boring."
2. ____ "Don't say that!"
3. ____ "I would like to have more grandchildren."
4. ____ "Rebecca and Ramón are friends?"
5. ____ "Don't be too sure."

## AFTER You Watch

**12** How much do you remember about the story? Check (✔) *True* or *False*.

|  | True | False |
|---|---|---|
| 1. The Mendozas want to go to Mexico for Christmas. | ____ | ____ |
| 2. Alice is the Mendozas' new friend. | ____ | ✔ |
| 3. The Mendozas and Alice talk about retirement. | ____ | ____ |
| 4. Mrs. Mendoza wants more grandchildren. | ____ | ____ |

**13** What do you know about Alice? Complete the sentences. Choose the answers.

1. __a__ Alice lives in __Phoenix, Arizona__.
   - **a.** Phoenix, Arizona
   - **b.** Los Angeles, California
   - **c.** Boston, Massachusetts

2. ____ Alice thinks retirement is _____.
   - **a.** exciting
   - **b.** boring
   - **c.** expensive

3. ____ Alice says Rebecca is _____.
   - **a.** thin
   - **b.** fat
   - **c.** funny

4. ____ Alice thinks Rebecca and Ramón are _____.
   - **a.** friends
   - **b.** more than friends
   - **c.** students

### What About YOU?

What is your opinion? Check (✔) *I agree* or *I disagree*.

|  | I agree | I disagree |
|---|---|---|
| 1. The Mendozas are nervous about retirement. | ____ | ____ |
| 2. Alice is a smart woman. | ____ | ____ |

# HIGHLIGHTS

## CULTURE

In the United States, Canada, and other countries, it is polite to make people feel comfortable at parties and meetings. For example, it is a good idea to speak a language that everyone understands.

Rebecca feels bad because she is not part of the conversation.

 **What can you do to make someone feel comfortable?**

You can _____ _____ .

## EXPRESSIONS

**14** Match the underlined words from the story with their meanings.

1. _____ not serious
2. _____ decide
3. ___c___ No thanks.
4. _____ find a solution

# REVIEW AND DISCUSS

## STORY SUMMARY

 **15** Use the words in the box to complete the story summary for Episode 23.

| dance | friend | ✔kitchen | Los Angeles | mother | parents |
| party | sad | school | speaks | thinks | understand |

Ramón talks to Alex in the ___kitchen___ (1). They talk about Alex's _____ (2). She is moving to _____ (3). Alex is _____ (4). He wants his _____ (5) to be together again. Rebecca sees Bill at _____ (6). She tells him about the retirement _____ (7). People sing and _____ (8) at the Mendozas' party. Rebecca meets Alberto's _____ (9), Gloria Díaz. Gloria _____ (10) Spanish with her friends. Rebecca doesn't _____ (11) her story. Rebecca also meets Alice Goodman. Alice _____ (12) Rebecca and Ramón are more than friends.

## VIEWPOINTS

**16** Watch the video discussion group. What does Roberto mean? Check (✔) *True* or *False*.

*I think that you can be in love with two people at the same time.*

Roberto Arévalo, Colombia

|  | True | False |
|---|---|---|
| 1. Roberto is talking about Mrs. Mendoza. | _____ | _____ |
| 2. Roberto thinks Rebecca loves Alberto and Ramón. | _____ | _____ |

 What is your opinion about Rebecca, Alberto, and Ramón? Circle your answers.

1. Ramón likes / loves Rebecca.
2. Alberto likes / loves Rebecca.
3. Rebecca likes / loves Ramón.
4. Rebecca likes / loves Alberto.

# THE PHONE CALL

EPISODE 24

**PREVIEW** In this episode, the Mendozas' retirement party continues. Rebecca gets bad news. She leaves the party early.

Rebecca and Alex at the party

1. Alex, is there something wrong?
2. I have to move with my mother to Los Angeles.

The Mendoza family at the party

Before we cut into this beautiful cake, a few words from the guests of honor…

Rebecca, Nancy, and Angela at the party

1. Your brother called. He said it was an emergency. He wants you to call him.
2. What is it?

## BEFORE You Watch

**1** **Look at the photos above. Circle the answers.**

1. Rebecca and Alex are at the (retirement party) / after-school program.
2. Alex is happy / sad about moving to Los Angeles.
3. The cake is for Alex / Mr. and Mrs. Mendoza.
4. Alberto wants his parents to speak / dance.
5. Nancy and Angela / Melaku give Rebecca a message from Kevin.
6. Kevin wants Rebecca to call him / write him a letter.

**Why is it difficult to move to a new city?**

It is difficult because _____.

…you miss your friends
…you miss your family
…you have to learn about a new place

# WATCH FOR MAIN IDEAS

Watch *all* of EPISODE 24, "The Phone Call."

## WHILE You Watch

**2** Who does Rebecca talk to at the party? Check (✔) their names.

1. ____✔____ Alex
2. _____ Ramón
3. _____ Mr. Mendoza
4. _____ Mrs. Mendoza
5. _____ Nancy
6. _____ Alberto
7. _____ Vincent
8. _____ Gloria Díaz

## AFTER You Watch

**3** How much do you remember about the story? Put the photos in order from 1 to 5.

a. _____
b. _____
c. _____
d. ____1____
e. _____

a.

b.

c.

d.

e.

## 4  What do you know about these people? Complete the sentences with the phrases below.

a. are retiring
✔ b. gets a present from Rebecca
c. is in the hospital
d. calls Kevin
e. tell Rebecca some bad news
f. dances with Rebecca

1. __b__ Alex __gets a present from Rebecca__.
2. _____ Rebecca _____.
3. _____ Ramón _____.
4. _____ Mr. and Mrs. Mendoza _____.
5. _____ Nancy and Angela _____.
6. _____ Rebecca's father _____.

## 5  What does Rebecca want to do? Check (✔) the sentence that *is not* true.

_____ a. Rebecca wants to go to Boston.
_____ b. Rebecca wants to stay at the party.
_____ c. Rebecca wants to see her brother.
_____ d. Rebecca wants to see her father.

 **What do you think will happen? Check (✔) Yes or No.**

|  | Yes | No |
|---|---|---|
| 1. Will Alberto and Ramón fight about Rebecca? | _____ | _____ |
| 2. Will Rebecca's father be OK? | _____ | _____ |
| 3. Will Rebecca be in Boston for a long time? | _____ | _____ |

EPISODE 24  page 3

# WATCH FOR DETAILS

 Watch PART 1.

## WHILE You Watch

**6** Who is speaking? Write **R** for *Rebecca*, **A** for *Alex*, or **M** for *Ramón Mendoza*.

1. __R__ "Your father told me."
2. _____ "I don't want to go."
3. _____ "What kind of surprise?"
4. _____ "Something my brother gave me."
5. _____ "Alex, now is the time."
6. _____ "Save me a dance."

## AFTER You Watch

**7** How much do you remember about the story? Complete the sentences. Choose the answers.

1. __b__ Alex wants to __stay in San Francisco__.
   a. move to Los Angeles    b. stay in San Francisco    c. live with Rebecca

2. _____ Alberto dances with _____.
   a. Rebecca    b. Gloria    c. his mother

3. _____ Rebecca gives Alex a _____.
   a. test    b. present    c. piano lesson

4. _____ Rebecca wants Alex to call her _____.
   a. Miss Casey    b. Coach    c. Rebecca

5. _____ Ramón wants to _____ with Rebecca.
   a. sit    b. talk    c. dance

 What do you like to do at parties? Complete the sentence. Check (✓) your answers.

I like to _____.

_____ talk        _____ eat

_____ dance      _____ watch people

EPISODE 24 page 4

## Watch PART 2.

## WHILE You Watch

**8** Listen to Mr. Mendoza's speech. Check (✔) the sentences he says.

1. ____✔____ "We wish to thank you all for coming. . . ."
2. _____ "We will never forget the good times. . . ."
3. _____ "To the greatest parents anyone ever had."
4. _____ ". . .the Mendoza tradition will continue."
5. _____ "Please eat, drink, and have fun."

## AFTER You Watch

**9** How much do you remember about the story? Check (✔) *True* or *False*.

|  | True | False |
|---|---|---|
| 1. Alberto helps make the cake. |  | ✔ |
| 2. Mr. and Mrs. Mendoza are retiring. |  |  |
| 3. Mr. and Mrs. Mendoza are selling the restaurant. |  |  |
| 4. Mrs. Mendoza is lucky to have her friends and her husband. |  |  |
| 5. Mrs. Mendoza cries at the party. |  |  |

**10** How does the Mendoza family feel about the restaurant? Circle the answers.

1. Mr. and Mrs. Mendoza love / hate it.
2. Alberto is happy / sad that his parents are not selling it.
3. Ramón is happy / sad that his parents are not selling it.

EPISODE 24 page 5

**Watch PART 3.**

## WHILE You Watch

**11** Listen to Nancy talk to Mr. Mendoza and Rebecca. Circle the words Nancy says.

1. "We're looking for Alberto Mendoza / (Rebecca Casey)."
2. "Your brother / father called."
3. "It's your aunt / father."
4. "He's in the hospital / apartment."

## AFTER You Watch

**12** How much do you remember about the story? Put the sentences in order from 1 to 5. Then write the sentences in the correct order below.

a. _____ Rebecca tells Ramón about her present to Alex.
b. _____ Rebecca leaves the party.
c. __1__ Ramón asks Rebecca to dance.
d. _____ Rebecca calls Kevin.
e. _____ Nancy and Angela tell Rebecca about her father.

1. _Ramón asks Rebecca to dance._
2. _____
3. _____
4. _____
5. _____

**13** What happens at the party? Check (✔) *Yes* or *No*.

|  | Yes | No |
|---|---|---|
| 1. Does Alberto see Ramón and Rebecca dance? | ____ | ____ |
| 2. Does Alberto dance with Rebecca? | ____ | ✔ |
| 3. Does Rebecca get bad news about her father? | ____ | ____ |
| 4. Does Rebecca leave with Nancy and Angela? | ____ | ____ |

**What About YOU?** What is your opinion? Check (✔) *I agree* or *I disagree*.

|  | I agree | I disagree |
|---|---|---|
| 1. Alberto is angry at Ramón. | ____ | ____ |
| 2. Rebecca isn't worried about her father. | ____ | ____ |

# HIGHLIGHTS

## CULTURE

**In the United States and Canada, most people retire after they work thirty or forty years.**

Many people want to relax when they retire.

Some people start new careers or hobbies.

 **What is your opinion? Check (✔) *True* or *False*.**

|   | True | False |
|---|---|---|
| 1. I want to relax when I retire. | _____ | _____ |
| 2. I want to retire when I am young. | _____ | _____ |
| 3. I want to retire when I am old. | _____ | _____ |

## EXPRESSIONS

 **Match the underlined words from the story with their meanings.**

1.

*I've got a little surprise for you to cheer you up.*

make you rich / make you happy

2.

*You know, Alex is crazy about you.*

really likes / doesn't understand

3.

*I'll take the next flight out... whatever it costs.*

next flight that leaves / most expensive flight

4.

*I'll pick up some clothes, and then we'll head to the airport.*

go to / talk at

EPISODE 24 page 7

# REVIEW AND DISCUSS

## STORY SUMMARY

**15** Use the words in the box to complete the story summary for Episode 24.

| bad | Boston | cake | calls | dances | father | friends |
|---|---|---|---|---|---|---|
| hospital | ✓ moving | parents | present | restaurant | sad | talk |

Alex is _____(1) about __moving__(2) to Los Angeles. Rebecca talks to him and gives him a _____(3). Ramón puts the _____(4) for his _____(5) on the table. Mr. and Mrs. Mendoza thank their _____(6). Mr. Mendoza says they will not sell the _____(7). Ramón _____(8) with Rebecca. They _____(9) about Alex. Nancy and Angela come to the restaurant. They have some _____(10) news for Rebecca. Her _____(11) is in the _____(12). Rebecca _____(13) Kevin. She needs to go to _____(14).

## VIEWPOINTS

**16** Watch the video discussion group. What does Boris mean? Check (✓) *True* or *False*.

> I would really react badly to something like that.

|  | True | False |
|---|---|---|
| 1. Boris is talking about Rebecca. | _____ | _____ |
| 2. Boris thinks it's hard to get news about a sick parent. | _____ | _____ |

**Boris Levitin, Russia**

### What About YOU?

How do you think Rebecca feels? Complete the sentence. Check (✓) your answers.

Rebecca is _____.

_____ angry      _____ sad
_____ relaxed    _____ scared
_____ happy      _____ worried

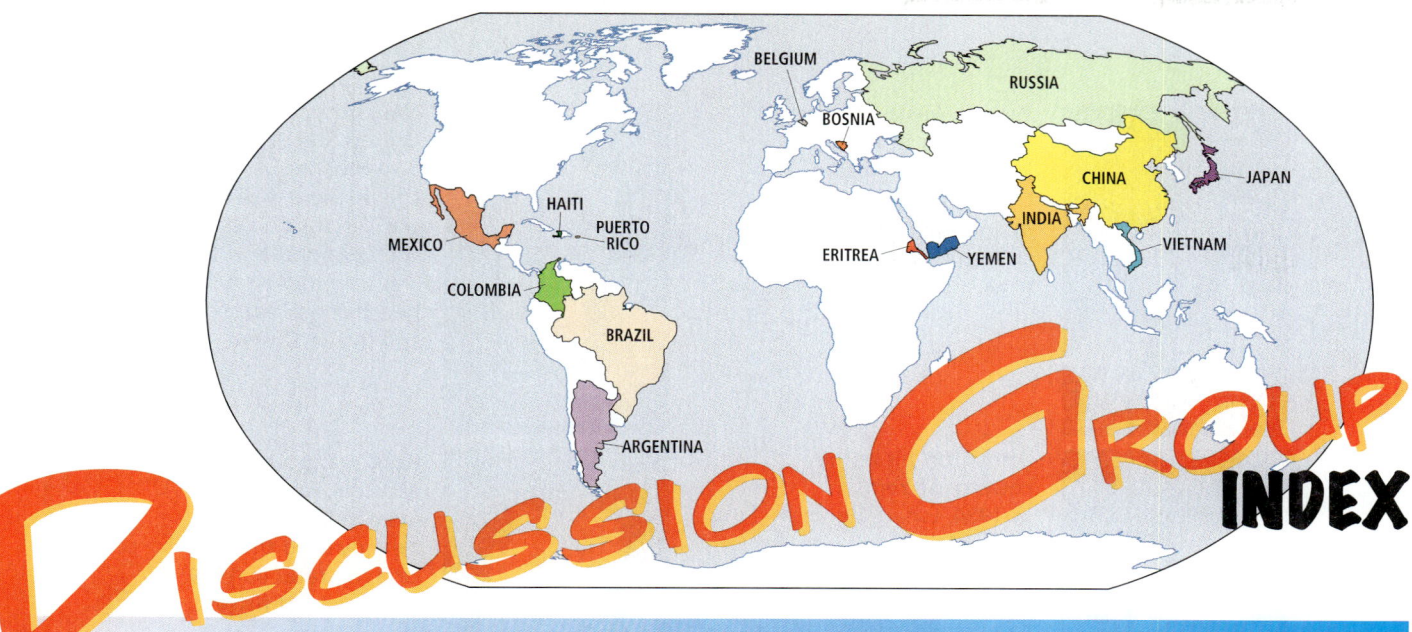

# Discussion Group Index

To find the students for the Discussion Group, signs about the CONNECT WITH ENGLISH television program were placed in universities and community centers in the Boston area. More than 100 people offered to participate. From this group, about 40 people auditioned on tape. They were asked questions like, "Where do you come from?" and, "How did you get to the United States?" The final 16 people were chosen because they told the most interesting stories, felt comfortable in front of the camera, and had clear speaking voices. The students did not have a script to read from. All of their stories are true, and they did not practice their lines.

**Roberto Arévalo
Colombia**

Roberto moved to the United States because he wanted to see more of the world. He arrived in 1981 and now works as a video producer. His wife is a doctor.

**Olga Baloueff
Belgium**

Olga lived in Belgium and in Zaire before she moved to the United States. She is currently going to graduate school in the Boston area, and she has a husband and a son.

**Nina Chen
China**

Nina was a teacher before she came to the United States in 1982. Nina thinks education is very important and is proud that both of her daughters have finished college.

**Ventha Danapalan
India**

Ventha came to the United States in 1992. Before he moved to Boston, he studied electrical engineering in Arizona.

**Laura Eastment
Argentina**

Laura moved to the United States from Argentina in 1969. She came to the United States to study agricultural engineering.

**Nisenat Gabrezgi
Eritrea**

Nisenat came to the United States in 1992. She says that her experiences in her new home are a lot like Rebecca's—except that Nisenat has the extra job of learning English!

DISCUSSION GROUP INDEX

**Patrick Jerome
Haiti**

Patrick was a filmmaker in Haiti before he moved to the United States in 1993. He attends college in the Boston area.

**Abdul Khushafah
Yemen**

Abdul left his home country of Yemen in 1984, where he worked as a carpenter. He is glad he made the decision to move. He now works as a designer.

**Lan Ma
China**

Lan is from Beijing, China, and came to the United States in 1990 to continue her education. When she arrived in Boston she didn't know anybody, but now she is very happy to live there.

**Casilda Nunes
Brazil**

Casilda is in the United States to study English. She only planned to stay for six months, but when the Discussion Group was filmed, she had been in the U.S. for almost two years.

**Hai B. Pho
Vietnam**

Hai arrived in the United States over forty years ago. His family wanted him to continue his education in the U.S. He moved back to Vietnam in the 1970s, but now he lives near Boston.

**Nela Hosic
Bosnia**

Nela had been in the United States only two months before she became a part of the Discussion Group. Her husband and two children moved with her, but her parents still live in Bosnia.

**Boris Levitin
Russia**

Boris was born in Moscow, Russia. He lived in Israel before he moved to the United States in 1979 at the age of fifteen.

**Raúl Méndez
Puerto Rico**

Raúl is a developmental psychologist at a hospital in Boston. He still works in Puerto Rico three months a year, and he has two grandchildren who live there.

**Yukiyoshi Ozawa
Japan**

Yukiyoshi was actually born in San Francisco, California, but he was raised in Japan. He is now a college student in Boston. He came to live in the United States in 1995.

**Rosalba Solís
Mexico**

Rosalba came from Mexico in 1978 to pursue her dream of becoming a jazz musician. Like Rebecca, she wanted to go to music school, and today she is a music teacher in Boston.

# Character Index

This index includes the names of most of the characters who appear in CONNECT WITH ENGLISH, alphabetized by their first names.

**Alberto Mendoza**
San Francisco, California. An architect who meets Rebecca in the desert.

**Alex Mendoza**
San Francisco, California. Ramón's son and a student at the after-school program.

**Angela Calud**
San Francisco, California. A nursing student. She lives at Nancy Shaw's house.

**Bill Ellis**
San Francisco, California. A student at the San Francisco College of Music and Rebecca's friend.

**Brendan & Anne Casey**
Aurora, Illinois. Rebecca and Kevin's uncle and aunt.

**Carmen & Enrique Mendoza**
San Francisco, California. Alberto and Ramón's parents. They own the Casa Mendoza restaurant.

**Edward Shaw**
San Francisco, California. A retired musician, he is Nancy Shaw's uncle. He lives in a nursing home.

**Emma Washington**
San Francisco, California. The director of the after-school program where Rebecca works.

**Frank Wells**
Boston, Massachusetts. Patrick Casey's friend.

**Jack Sullivan**
Boston, Massachusetts. Sandy's boyfriend.

**Kevin Casey**
Boston, Massachusetts. Patrick Casey's son and Rebecca's younger brother.

**María Gómez**
San Francisco, California. The financial aid counselor at the San Francisco College of Music.

CHARACTER INDEX

**Matt Carlson**
Boston, Massachusetts. Rebecca's boyfriend in Boston.

**Melaku Tadesse**
San Francisco, California. A business student. He lives at Nancy Shaw's house.

**Molly Kelly**
Boston, Massachusetts. Margaret Casey's sister, and Rebecca and Kevin's aunt.

**Nancy Shaw**
San Francisco, California. Rebecca's godmother. She runs a boarding house for students. Rebecca lives with her in San Francisco.

**Patrick Casey**
Boston, Massachusetts. Rebecca and Kevin's father. He is a retired firefighter.

**Ramón Mendoza**
San Francisco, California. Alex's father and Alberto's brother. He works at his parents' restaurant.

**Rebecca Casey**
Boston, Massachusetts and San Francisco, California. A music student with a dream. She moves from Boston to San Francisco to study music. She is Patrick's daughter and Kevin's older sister.

**Sandy Dawson**
Boston, Massachusetts. Rebecca's best friend and Jack's girlfriend.

**Professor Thomas**
San Francisco, California. One of Rebecca's professors at the San Francisco College of Music.

**Mr. & Mrs. Wang**
San Francisco, California. Vincent's parents. Mr. Wang owns a store in Chinatown.

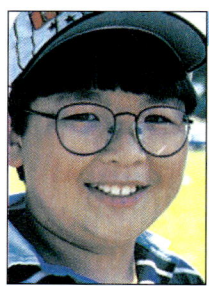
**Vincent Wang**
San Francisco, California. Alex's best friend at the after-school program. He is the son of Mr. and Mrs. Wang.